Indoor Games and Activities

A comprehensive guide to
the teaching of games skills to pupils
of seven to thirteen years

Alison L. Parratt

HODDER AND STOUGHTON
LONDON   SYDNEY   AUCKLAND   TORONTO

Acknowledgment

My thanks to Daphne T. and Jean G. for their typing,
Wendy K. for her photography and Sue C. for her
encouragement.

British Library Cataloguing in Publication Data
Parratt, Alison L.
  Indoor games and activities.
  1. Indoor games
  I. Title
  793'.024372   GV1229

ISBN 0 340 32400 7

First published 1983

Printed and bound in Great Britain for
Hodder and Stoughton Educational,
a division of Hodder and Stoughton Ltd,
Mill Road, Dunton Green, Sevenoaks, Kent,
by Biddles Ltd, Guildford, Surrey.

Set in 11/12 point Plantin (Linotron) by
Rowland Phototypesetting Ltd, Bury St Edmunds, Suffolk.

Contents

Introduction

The winter months provide limited opportunity for the younger children to take their games lessons outside. To ensure a continuation of the learning process, despite the restrictions imposed by frequent indoor lessons, it is useful to offer a wide range of interesting and challenging activities which will provide the necessary groundwork for development.

In the following chapters a comprehensive selection of games and activities for indoor use, by both the class and specialist teacher, has been compiled for easy reference and guidance. The selection is primarily aimed at the Junior and Middle school age groups (7–13) who are often the most likely to be affected by adverse weather conditions. Many of the suggested practices for individual partner and group work can also be used for lessons outside, whether on tarmac or grass.

Due to the wide choice of activities, and the extensive range and variety of small apparatus used, it is relatively easy to choose practices suitable for any type of indoor area with large groups of children actively involved in some form of worthwhile exercise.

The teaching of such lessons needs thought and organisation to avoid large team groups offering little actual participation for the individual. It is always important to remember that on those inclement days when children are often confined to classrooms they have a tremendous amount of excess energy to release, and the games lesson should provide the outlet through vigorous exercise.

Within the confines of the most uninspiring surroundings it is possible to involve *all* the children in a variety of different tag games. Children should also be given the opportunity of working with an assortment of equipment ranging from hoops, ropes, to balls, bats, and so on.

If children are expected to obtain any acceptable level of proficiency in sport generally, the basic foundations on which their progress must develop have got to be extensive. By building this broad framework of progressive skills, more structured and competitive activities will develop into small games, providing the necessary transition to major games later.

With the rapid growth of leisure facilities available to children and adults alike, it is becoming increasingly more important that this early opportunity is used to train children in a selection of skills for immediate and later use, at the same time creating an enjoyable memory and a healthy attitude towards sport generally.

Unfortunately this is not always the approach adopted, as the easy solution to coping with an indoor lesson seems to be to arrange children into large groups with a limited repertoire of team games repeated from one lesson to the next. Usually discipline suffers under such conditions as the activity is often boring and offers very limited participation for each child.

However, with the increasing demands forced upon teachers, little spare time is available for the non-specialist to learn how to improve standards of teaching the many aspects of physical education. Under these circumstances it is little wonder that development in training appears to take a back seat, with the imagination and interest of the children rarely being used to their full advantage.

During indoor lessons it is necessary to remember the essential principles which apply to this type of learning situation:
—*enjoyment* combined with maximum participation for *all* the children;
—*opportunities* for children to experience a variety of skills and equipment;
—*instructions* kept to a minimum, with the children learning by doing;
—*co-operation*, with children learning to work with others;
—*responsibility* for own appearance and equipment, promoting the need for self-control and respect for property.

As with any games teaching, the organisation of an indoor lesson should follow the basic plan set out below:
(a) *Warm up* – introductory activities or tag games (Chapter 1);
(b) *Skills practices*, individually then in pairs (Chapters 2, 3);
(c) *Group practices* based on individual work (Chapters 4, 5);
(d) *Game situation* – whether 2 v 2 or 15 v 15 (Chapters 5, 6).

By selecting one or more practices from each of the six chapters in this book, lessons suitable to individual facilities may be created to follow this suggested lesson plan.

This basic framework does however allow for flexibility. In order to accommodate practices requiring more space, or those where equipment is limited, the usual method of all the class attempting skills at the same time can be adapted to suit the conditions. Under these circumstances it is a good idea to arrange the children into small groups, each of which is allocated a different activity. Then by the teacher rotating the groups, each individual child still has the opportunity of experiencing a variety of skills.

A large dot ● in the margin indicates more advanced and taxing activities.

Throughout this type of teaching situation the three elements which should always be present are *enjoyment*, *activity*, and *learning*. With these important points kept in mind and combined with ideas from the different chapters, the standard of teaching and level of pupil attainment will without doubt improve.

Sportsmanship

The players' approach to any skills practice, activity, or game, depends on the standards set by the school, and the attitudes of staff directly involved. Outside influences are greater than ever, with the media often highlighting the so called 'professional foul', giving P.E. teachers generally a wider responsibility to ensure high standards of sportsmanship, discipline and dress.

Teachers must constantly be aware of the need for players not only to perfect their skills, but also to adopt the right manner when they play. Emphasis should not be constantly placed on the winning individual or team, but also on the less able child who has achieved greater success by mastering a new and difficult skill.

Children also need to be taught how to accept victory, avoiding over-reaction, and how to cope with defeat without feeling a failure. Too often children are exposed to unnecessary pressures from both parents and staff who see defeat as a disgrace and failure.

Sport should be fun, something for all the children to enjoy and participate in. Once this enjoyment is established the learning process will be accelerated and the players will feel a real need for the establishment of standards and rules to enable further progress to be made. Players dislike the over-confident winner or the cheat, and if teachers educate their children in the etiquette of sport a much healthier attitude and approach will emerge.

Dress

It is essential that children are suitably attired for the activity undertaken, to enable freedom of movement and to ensure the maximum ofsafety.

Preferably the children should change before and after lessons, removing all items of jewellery in order to prevent damage or injury to themselves or others.

Hygiene

Most of the practices and games can be attempted by children working bare-footed, but if this is the case, there will be a need for regular checks to ensure children are not suffering from any type of foot infection.

If shower facilities are available these should be utilised and children encouraged to take a pride in their appearance and be aware of the need for bathing or showering after exercise.

Refereeing and Umpiring

For mini-games it is often quite useful to appoint referees/ umpires from amongst the players, with the teacher first explaining and establishing a common code of rules and a simple scoring system. This then allows for several games to be played simultaneously with teams maintaining a uniform approach and establishing fair play. This additional restriction on the game also makes the children more aware of the need to discipline themselves as they learn to work together within the guidelines of the rules.

Safety and Organisation

This aspect of any indoor organised activity needs careful and continual thought and consideration. The teacher should never be afraid to stop children and re-organise or re-arrange the activity in the interests of safety. Prevention is always better than cure.

For individual skills and activities, good spacing of the children is vital and any dangers, e.g. projecting fixtures, should be pointed out to the children as hazards to be avoided if it is not possible to remove them.

Where an activity involves a great deal of movement (e.g. tag games) it is essential to emphasise the need for children to run forwards and sideways – never backwards into others or a wall. Also if children are required to link hands to form a chain, ensure there is adequate space to accommodate the size of the chain without there being an unnecessary safety risk.

To ensure the maximum safety in a crowded situation it may be a necessary precaution to limit the skills and games to those using just a ball – preferably foam. However an alternative to this would be to organise several groups working on different activities, confining the bat and stick practices to small groups of children. This idea is very useful for those teaching in schools where only limited numbers of equipment are available.

Storage

Equipment can also be a danger if left to clutter the playing area, highlighting the constant need to store apparatus in suitable containers, out of the way when not in immediate use. The children should be encouraged to respect any equipment, with the teacher demonstrating and explaining how it is best handled and stored.

At the end of a lesson ensure all the apparatus has been correctly stored and report any loss or damage to the teacher responsible for this area of the curriculum. This is a useful procedure which, if adopted by all, could save time at the beginning of lessons and money on replacing faulty or lost items.

Activities for the handicapped child

Many activities described in the following chapters can be adapted to meet the specific needs of children who suffer from physical handicaps, e.g. cerebral palsy, deafness, spinal paralysis, or amputation.

The nature and degree of the disability will obviously influence the choice of activity and determine the way in which it can be developed. But it is equally important that the handicapped child should be given the same opportunities as the able-bodied in the acquisition of skills.

Throughout all activities the safety of the individual must be the major consideration when selecting and organising games. However this very necessary precaution should not deter involvement in sport but encourage teachers to think of ways of adapting the skills and practices to meet the special needs of these children.

Equipment

Foam balls in a variety of sizes and bounce qualities (low, medium and high bounce) must be the safest, most versatile type of ball suitable for use by handicapped children, requiring little effort to propel and handle because of their composition. However, it is still important to provide lightweight plastic and airflow balls for the children to work with once they have mastered the basic skills of throwing, catching, striking and kicking.

An alternative item of equipment for the children to throw and catch is the beanbag. This can prove easier to handle than a ball because of its flexible shape.

Any striking implements used would be best selected from the lighter, more durable range of plastic or polypropylene bats, rackets and sticks, the handle of which may have to be altered according to the type of disability.

Using the selection of equipment mentioned above, most activities outlined in the six chapters present little difficulty for the handicapped child to attempt, provided that playing areas are modified to allow participants some degree of success.

Note: Any high targets (netball, basketball rings and so on) need to be lowered to an appropriate height. Floor targets should be larger with the shooting distance reduced, nets should be lowered and goal areas increased in size. Once sufficient skill has been gained by the children, the goals and targets can be repositioned to develop the standard of play.

I
Tag Games

It is most important to stress the constant need for players to look where they are going, to avoid others, and not to travel backwards.

1 **Chain tag** One or two children are given bands and act as catchers. Once players are caught, they join hands with the catchers, gradually making a chain of catchers. The size of the chain can be restricted to a maximum of three children per chain, so that when a fourth child is caught the chain splits up to make two chains of two catchers.

2 **Individual tag** One child is catcher, and whoever is caught is then the new catcher.

3 **Partner tag** Catchers work in twos, holding inside hands. When either catcher tags a player, the catcher is freed and is replaced by the person caught.

4 **Stuck-in-the-mud** One or two children are given bands and act as catchers. Once a player is caught, he/she stands still with arms out and legs apart. To release the player 'stuck-in-the-mud', someone who is free crawls between his/her legs.

Variations: (i) Release by running under arms. (ii) A player who is caught crouches down and is released by a free player jumping over him/her.

5 **Tail tag** Every player has a band to tuck into the back of the shorts like a tail. Once the instruction is given, children try to prevent people taking their own tails while collecting the tails of others. The winner is either the last child to lose his/her own tail, or the child who collects most tails. (*Note*: Children must not hold their own tails in place.)

6 **Partner tail tag** Working in twos, one child has a tail and the partner tries to take it. The child defends the tail by dodging sideways, *never* backwards.

7 **Group tail tag** Working in threes or fours, one child has a tail and the others try to take it.
Variation: Circle tail tag (see diagram)

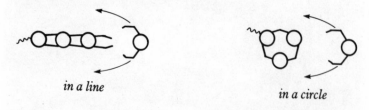

in a line   *in a circle*

1 Group tail tag

8 **Partner tag** Working in twos, one child has to try to tag his/her own partner who then becomes the catcher, and so the process is repeated.

9 **All-in-tag** One catcher wears a band, and anyone caught also gets a band and helps to catch the remaining players.

10 **Ball tag** Using a lightweight (foam) ball, the catcher tags runners by throwing the ball to hit them below the knee. Those caught may be released in similar ways to those suggested under *4 Stuck-in-the-mud*, or by a second player with a ball who repeats the actions of the catcher.

11 **Partner tag with equipment** While bouncing a small ball, a player chases a partner (giving a couple of metres start).
Variations: (i) Use a larger ball (netball). (ii) Dribble a ball with the feet. (iii) Use a stick to dribble a small ball. (iv) Bounce a small ball using a bat. (v) Hit a small ball in the air using a bat. (vi) Skip. (vii) Throw and catch a bean bag. (viii) Use a quoit as in (vii). These variations require a little more space. They can also be adapted to *2 Individual tag*.

12 **Chinese wall** The catcher stands in a central area between two lines. Children try to cross this area without being caught. Once caught, they join the catcher in the middle until eventually all the children are caught.

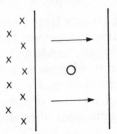

Children try to cross the central area without being tagged by the catcher.

2 Chinese wall

13 **Lines** Children run or jump over any lines. When the teacher blows the whistle, the last child standing on a line loses a life.
Variation: Substitute mats or hoops for lines.

14 **Trains/buses** Travelling round the hall in 4s, play follow-my-leader. On the whistle, all groups race to their own station (hoop, mat, chalk mark). The first train/bus home gets a point, or the last home loses a life.
Variations: As above, but give the four sides of the hall the name of a station. Instead of using a whistle, call out the name of a station and score as above.

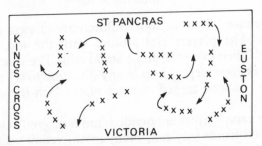

The groups travel round the room, lining up at the appropriate station when the command is given.

3 Trains/Buses

15 **Jack Frost and the Sun** Jack Frost wearing a blue band freezes the children when he catches them; the Sun wearing a yellow band releases them.

16 **Safety Tag** Use mats or chalk circles well spaced around the floor area. One catcher chases the other children who cannot be tagged while standing on a mat or in a circle. The catcher changes places each time with the player who has been tagged.

17 **Circle release tag** Draw a large circle in the middle of the floor or join several mats together. Divide the class into two teams. One team wears bands and are catchers. When a member of the non-band team is tagged, he/she is taken to stand in the central area and must remain there unless released by another member of the team who has not yet been caught. The game ends when all the non-band team are in the centre.

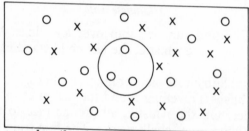

x *catchers (bands)*
O *non-bands*

Non-bands who are tagged are put in the catcher's circle and can only be released by a free team-mate.

4 Circle release tag

18 **Step chase** Three or four children are chasers and wear bands. The players run around until the teacher calls, 'Stop!' Then everyone must stand still. The catchers may then take one step or leap in any direction to try to catch a player. Anyone tagged changes places with the successful catcher.

19 **Home race** Players are divided into four groups and given coloured bands (say red, blue, green, yellow). Each team has its own home area in a corner (mats, chalk circles, or similar). All groups travel round the room in a manner specified by the teacher, and in a clockwise direction. At a signal the players travel to their own home area as fast as they can. The first team home can be awarded a point, or the last home can lose a life. The travelling movement can be changed each time (e.g. hop, skip, crawl, and so on).

20 **Concentration** Children run round the hall until the teacher calls out a number. Whatever the number, children must then gather into groups of that number. Those not in a group of the correct number must drop out.
Variation: The children may travel round in a variety of different ways and be encouraged to freeze when in the correct groupings. Anyone who moves after that is out. Additional tasks may be set (e.g. in threes, lifting one off the ground; in twos, standing back to back). Children really have to concentrate to avoid being out, hence the name of the game.

21 **Mat or hoop tag** Mats or hoops are spread all over the floor quite close together. One player (wearing a band) is the chaser while all the children start to move from mat to mat, or hoop to hoop. If anyone steps off a mat he/she must stand still and count up to 10 before moving on. Whoever is then caught either becomes the new catcher or an additional one.

22 **Back to back** Children stand back to back with a partner of similar size and link arms. Catchers wearing bands adopt the same position and co-ordinate their legs to travel sideways trying to tag other pairs who must move in a similar way to stay free. If pairs lose contact with one another they are automatically caught. This game may then be organised in a variety of ways similar to individual, all-in, release tag, and Jack Frost.

2
Individual Skills

For children to gain full enjoyment from a game it must be played with some degree of skill. It is therefore necessary to provide the opportunity for acquiring and practising the relevant skills within the framework of the games lesson even if it is held indoors. In this way a new game can be introduced more successfully and games already familiar can be tackled with improved skill, higher standards being attained. Match play should not be allowed to dominate games teaching, with the educational needs of the many being sacrificed for the success of the few.

Throughout the individual work described in this chapter, it is important to provide challenging and often competitive situations which the children should be encouraged to attempt with both right and left hands or feet, according to the task.

Within the context of individual work, a wide range of experience should be made available to the children, providing them with the opportunity to tackle the basic skills using a variety of different shaped and sized balls, bats, rackets and sticks. Thus is established a broad foundation on which practices relating to minor and major games can later be developed.

Apparatus available

The selection of equipment suggested for use in the activities and games described in this book is listed below under the main headings *balls, bats, sticks, rackets,* and *miscellany.* (A comprehensive list of suitable equipment appears on page 131.)

Balls (airflow, foam, tennis, pudding, netball sizes 4–5, football sizes 3–5, Rugby sizes 4–5, volleyball, basketball, and lightweight plastic footballs)
The foam ball, available from tennis to football size and in three bounce qualities, high, medium, and low, is a relative newcomer to the sports scene and heralds a major breakthrough in indoor equipment. Made from a solid piece of lightweight foam it is completely safe for use in restricted areas, whether with sticks, bats, or rackets (even badminton rackets). It may also be hit against glass, brick or wooden walls and partitions without any fear of damage. Thus it can be used for a wide variety of skills and activities without the constant worry of injury or damage in a restricted or crowded situation.

Bats
Plywood cut-out bats are suitable for most of the work and these come in a variety of sizes and shapes, based on cricket, padder tennis and table tennis bats. More sophisticated bats incorpor-

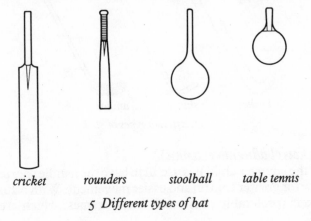

cricket   rounders   stoolball   table tennis

5 *Different types of bat*

ating built-up handles may also be used if available, but not only are they heavier to manoeuvre, they are also more costly, and the cheaper bats are perfectly adequate for this type of use. The exception is the rounders bat which because of its cylindrical shape is impossible to create in a cheaper plywood form. However, most schools have a supply of rounders bats in sufficient quantity for the needs of the indoor lesson.

A new range of good quality plastic and polypropylene equipment is also appearing on the market, offering a light-weight and durable alternative to the wooden shapes.

Sticks (shinty, hockey, unihoc)

The shinty stick made from wood is cheap and resembles a walking stick. However, a greater degree of skill is required in controlling a ball with this stick than with others, owing to its thin head.

The hockey stick is available in a range of sizes, but the head should be covered with a sock for protection of both stick and floor surface during indoor activities.

Being plastic, the unihoc stick will not damage the floor. However, the flat-bladed head of the stick enables children to use both sides of it (which of course is not allowed in hockey).

Although quite expensive, the new polypropylene sticks are the ideal choice for indoor work as they resemble wooden sticks but will not damage floor surfaces.

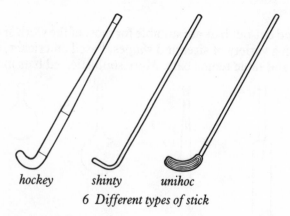

hockey   shinty   unihoc

6 *Different types of stick*

Rackets (badminton, tennis)

For the younger child it is useful to have the handle shortened to allow for greater control and easier movement. With badminton rackets (preferably those with metal frames, which are more hardwearing than wood and will not warp) it is possible to use both shuttlecocks and foam balls (tennis ball size), enabling two games to be practised with the same racket. The shorter-handled plastic rackets available are also very useful for smaller children when used with a small foam ball.

Miscellany (hoops, quoits, skipping ropes, bean-bags, skittles)
Plastic hoops (available in different sizes) can be used both as apparatus for the children to work with and as useful targets.

Skittles come in various sizes and composition; they may be made from plastic, wood, or plastic-coated wire. All types are very versatile; they can be used to create static targets, to support canes to provide improvised nets, to provide obstacles for players to negotiate, to mark goals, and to support hoops either horizontally or vertically.

Individual skills

Footwork
Footwork skills can be practised in many different ways:
(a) running and jumping and changing direction when the whistle is blown;
(b) running and jumping – freezing when the whistle is blown;
(c) dodging in and out of everyone else, who must not be touched (gradually reduce the space, with those touched having to stand still);
(d) running and jumping high in the air, as if catching a ball, when the whistle is blown (remembering to land carefully and stay still);
(e) as (d) but turning so as to land facing in a different direction;
(f) travelling round the area, jumping over any mats, hoops, or lines (vary the activity by encouraging children to jump in different ways – from one foot to land on two, or from two feet to land on two, or even to hop over obstacles).

To increase the height jumped, bands may be suspended from netball rings, or any suitable available fixtures, and children encouraged to jump and touch them.

Footwork for netball may be introduced if working with girls, including pivoting on the landing foot which should not move from the spot. This skill may be practised in many of the activities suggested above.

Individual skills with apparatus

Tennis or foam ball skills

(a) **Bouncing** Children bounce the ball using first the right and then the left hand, with competition being introduced by stating a specific number of bounces (e.g. 20 bounces). The task may then be repeated using alternate hands to bounce the ball, or aiming at a specific chalk mark or line on the floor, counting the number of accurate bounces out of 20.

Keeping the feet still, bounce the ball right round the body, changing hands when necessary. Then progress to a figure of eight with players bouncing the ball in and out of their own feet which are placed apart on the floor (see diagram).

round the body   *in a figure of eight round the feet*

7 *Individual bouncing skills*

(b) **Batting** Children use the flat of the hand as a bat. They should use first the right hand and then the left hand, then try alternate hands as with the bouncing skills.

allowing one bounce   *keeping the ball in the*   *using alternate hands*
between hits   *air using one hand only*

8 *Individual batting skills*

For those children who have difficulty co-ordinating this particular movement, it is simpler if the ball is allowed to bounce between each hit. This exercise may also be tried against a wall or other similar surface, allowing the ball to bounce between each return and encouraging children to use both hands. The more skilful performers can try to aim for a specific mark or circle.

Note: To increase hand mobility and co-ordination, the batting skills may be developed even further. Using one hand, children try to keep a rally going, using first the palm and then the back of the hand alternately for each hit. The skill may then be tried with the other hand. A competitive element may be introduced: who can (i) be the first to complete 10 hits; (ii) be the one to do the most hits in succession?

This skill leads on to the use of the side or edge of the fingers which requires much concentration and provides a real challenge for children. Where ability allows, this particular task may be combined with the previous one using both sides of the hand. Progress to batting the ball first with the palm, then the side, then the back of the hand, trying to keep this sequence of hitting going.

(c) **Throwing and catching** This basic skill practice can commence with the children throwing the ball in the air and using both hands for catching. Develop this important skill by increasing the height of each throw and also by restricting catching to the right or left hand only. If real difficulty is experienced, allow the ball to bounce before it is caught. Also encourage children to catch the ball above their heads as well as at waist height in front of the body, and to use both right and left hands not only for catching but throwing too.

Note: Throughout this activity the children will need frequent reminders to watch the ball and reach out for it and pull it in when caught.

Using a wall or similar surface, use both hands initially for throwing and catching a ball. This skill may be developed in a number of ways to increase the degree of difficulty. The distance from the wall may be increased and the children restricted to using one hand, or alternating

scoring   ■ ● ✕   scoring

non-scoring

9 *Target areas can be drawn on a wall, or on a card to be attached to a wall.*

between right and left. It may also be possible to introduce a second ball into this skills activity.

Target areas on the wall also increase the difficulty while providing the means for creating a competition. Variations are allowing the ball to bounce before being caught or by bouncing the ball against the floor before it hits the wall (see diagram).

using one ball and a wall

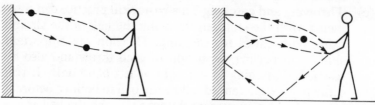

using two balls and a wall
10 Throwing and catching practices

For the combined skills of ball work and suppleness/flexibility, many of these activities may be developed to include the child's own body as an obstacle (e.g. throwing the ball under the raised right leg and trying to catch it after one bounce, then before it bounces). This activity should be attempted first with two-handed and eventually with one-hand catching, using the right and the left leg to form a sequence or pattern of movements.

For a twisting movement, children should be encouraged to try using their right hands, throwing the ball round their backs into the air on the left side, trying to catch it after one bounce, then trying to catch it before it bounces. This fun-skill can be developed for use with both right and left hands, and eventually restricted to throwing and catching with the same hand.

(d) **Dribbling** Using both feet the children can dribble a ball freely round the area. More specific tasks can be set by limiting children to the use of first the right and then the left foot, encouraging use of both the inside and outside of the foot. For improved control, children stop the ball when the teacher blows the whistle, or for greater variety still an additional skill can be included, e.g. bouncing the ball ten times, with the first child finished gaining a point, then continuing the dribbling activity. In this way an element of competition is introduced.

Obstacles such as hoops, ropes, mats, bean-bags, or even chalk marks can also provide an exciting challenge for each child to negotiate.

(e) **Juggling** Using the top of the toes, the children try to keep the ball in the air, letting it bounce once between each kick. From this, develop the use of alternate feet to keep the ball going, and eventually (where ability allows) these skills may be attempted without the ball bouncing at all.

The top of the knee may be used in exactly the same way as the toes, following the procedure described above. Then a combination sequence of the two skills can be developed,

Using the top of the toes, let the ball bounce once between each touch.

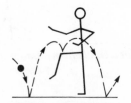

as above, but using the knee

combined heading and foot juggling

11 Juggling skills

providing a more difficult task for the talented and older pupils. Heading may also be included in this collection of individual activities (allow the ball to bounce initially). All the above juggling skills can be linked with catching – e.g. flick the ball in the air using the top of the toes and try to catch it after, and eventually before, it has bounced.

Skills with a football

The dribbling and juggling skills and activities for tennis or foam ball described above are all suitable for use with a lightweight football size 3, 4, or 5, or even a large foam ball.

Competition may be introduced throughout the various practices thus: (a) who can dribble to a set line first; (b) who can toe-juggle a ball the longest; (c) who can head a ball five consecutive times, and so on.

In addition to juggling and dribbling skills, passing, trapping and throw-ins can be practised. Using a wall, or a bench turned on its side, children can push the ball (using the inside of the foot) and then trap or stop the rebounding ball (again using the inside of the foot or leg). Speed and accuracy in this particular skill can be improved with the use of targets at which to aim – e.g. the first child to score five hits becomes the winner.

The throw-in action can be practised using a mark already existing on the floor, or adapting a suitable alternative (chalk mark, skipping rope). Accuracy and distance may be improved by placing targets (hoops or mats) on the floor, with a suitable scoring system for every successful throw-in. By introducing the use of a wall, it is also possible to practise trapping the ball on its rebound from the throw-in. This calls for quick reactions.

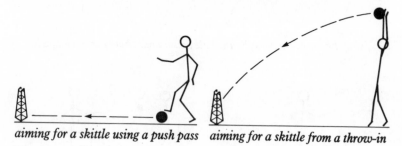

aiming for a skittle using a push pass   *aiming for a skittle from a throw-in*

trapping the rebound from a throw-in

12 Football

Skills with a netball

As they did with the tennis ball, children can easily practise throwing and catching a netball in the air and also against a suitable wall. The latter practice may include the different types of passes: chest, bounce, overhead, shoulder, and underarm (diagram 13), and the degree of accuracy can be improved by

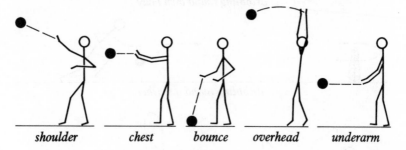

| shoulder | chest | bounce | overhead | underarm |

13 Netball passes

using targets placed on the floor or wall. In addition, it is also possible for children to practise shooting into goals permanently fixed to walls, or into portable units or even into hoops suspended from fittings or held by a partner. All these skills can be made into challenging and competitive situations: (a) who can be the first to do 20 chest passes against the wall; (b) who can be the first to hit the target area on the wall 10 times; (c) who can do the most shoulder passes against the wall in 30 seconds.

Skills with a basketball

Its similarity to netball enables many of the skills from the above section to be adapted for basketball. The throws, however, need to be confined to bounce, chest, and overhead, which can only really be practised against a wall, with the introduction of targets for improved accuracy.

The important skill of dribbling with a basketball (bouncing the ball with the fingertips) can easily be practised when the child is either stationary or travelling, and there are numerous ways in which this can be attempted, including simple competitive situations. Try dribbling:
(a) the ball round the player's own body without stopping;
(b) the ball in a figure of eight round the player's own feet;
(c) when racing to a set marker, trying to beat the rest of the class;
(d) following a straight line marked on the floor;

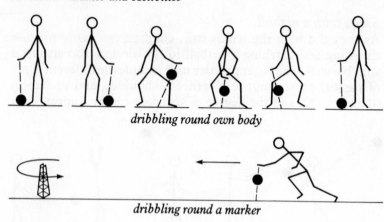

dribbling round own body

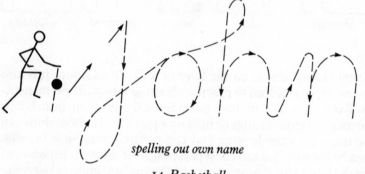

dribbling round a marker

spelling out own name

14 Basketball

(e) spelling out the player's own name in large, joined-up writing.

Shooting from a stationary position, and from dribbling, may also be attempted using improvised goals (as suggested in the netball section above).

Skills with a volleyball

The balls used for this type of activity need to be lightweight and well pumped up. The introduction to this sport should involve the child in trying to pat the ball up into the air, letting it bounce between each hit. The use of the lower forearms to strike the ball should gradually be substituted for the initial flat-handed smacking action. This basic way of playing the ball into the air is technically called a 'dig'.

The second action involves using the finger tips to keep the ball in the air above the head, the 'volley'. Both these actions can initially be practised allowing the ball to bounce. Eventually

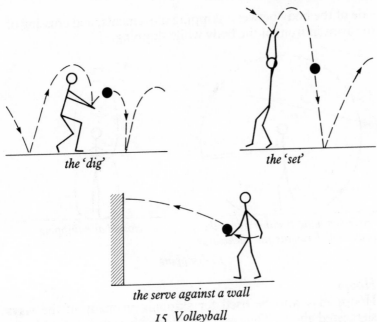

the 'dig'

the 'set'

the serve against a wall

15 Volleyball

attempts should be made to keep the ball in the air and off the floor.

The 'serving action' of hitting the ball with the heel of one hand underarm may also be practised individually, and the addition of a chalk mark at net height on a wall provides for more accurate practising. This can also be used for children trying the dig and volley action – to ensure the ball is gaining sufficient height.

Skipping ropes

Lay the skipping rope out on the floor and encourage children to try to jump its full length. The rope, if held loosely in front of the body with hands about two feet apart, will also provide an obstacle to be jumped over by the child holding the rope.

Encourage children to skip forwards and backwards on the spot with and without a second bounce between each complete circle of the rope. Children may also use both feet, alternate feet, and eventually hop, with challenges made to trigger the enthusiasm of the class (e.g. who can do 20 skips first, or who can keep going the longest when turning the rope backwards?).

All these aspects of skipping may be adapted for use on the move (if space allows), with the addition of rope swinging either side of the body between skipping movements, and crossing of the arms in front of the body while skipping.

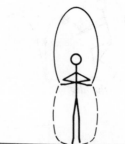

rope-swinging on either side of the body, both forwards and backwards

crossed arm skipping

16 *Skipping*

Hoops

Hoops may also be used for skipping in many of the ways suggested above. They also provide an obstacle for climbing in and out of, as well as for swinging, rolling, spinning, hula-hooping, and throwing and catching. Additional tasks may be set while a skill is tackled: e.g. how many times can you run round a spinning hoop before it stops? Can you race your rolling hoop across the room? Can you hit a skittle/large ball with a rolling hoop?

Hula-hooping may provide an opportunity for light-hearted activities: e.g. can you hula-hoop with your middle, arm, both legs, one at a time? These types of activities can be tried with hoops of varying sizes if they are available.

Beanbags

The beanbag is an old-fashioned but very useful item of equipment which has endless possibilities, particularly for the younger or physically handicapped child who experiences difficulty in grasping a ball. Like a small ball, a beanbag can easily be used for throwing and catching in the air, first using both hands, then the right hand, then the left only (see under *Throwing and catching*, page 17, for more details).

Because of its versatile shape, the beanbag can be placed between the knees or the ankles, and children encouraged to move around the room as fast as they can. This activity can also be attempted with a beanbag balanced on the head. Accuracy

may be practised by sliding the beanbag along the ground to hit
an object (a skittle, say), or throwing it to land on a target (chalk
mark, hoop, and so on).

Quoits

Quoits provide a different shape with which children can
experience the basic throwing, catching and aiming skills.

All the suggested activities for beanbags, and some of those
suggested for tennis ball throwing and catching practices can be
adapted for quoit work.

Children can also try juggling with two quoits which they
may find easier to control than balls. As well as sliding a quoit
for accuracy, a more difficult skill to practise is to roll it, or to try
to hook it over a skittle or a rounders post.

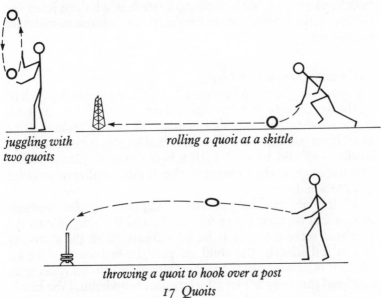

*juggling with
two quoits*

rolling a quoit at a skittle

throwing a quoit to hook over a post

17 Quoits

Skills with a bat and ball

This type of skills practice should try to offer a wide range of
balls and bat shapes – e.g. airflow, foam and tennis balls, with
cricket, padder tennis, stoolball and table tennis bat shapes.

Many of the activities suitable for this equipment are adapta-
tions of those explained under *Batting*, page 88.

Probably the easiest introduction to this type of practice is to
bounce the ball on the floor using the bat, encouraging accuracy
and an increase of speed by competition (e.g. who can be the

first to bounce the ball 20 times, to bounce the ball on a chalk mark, or similar target, 10 times, and so on).

This type of practice should be done holding the bat with first one hand and then the other. Children should progress to keeping the ball in the air by hitting it with the bat after one bounce, then hitting it before it bounces. It is then possible to combine these movements to form a challenging sequence demanding both skill and concentration.

Target areas created on a wall or similar surface can be used to increase the difficulty of the practices and offer the opportunity to create competitions. The player throws the ball in the air and allows it to bounce before hitting it against the wall. The rebound ball is also allowed to bounce before it is hit again. Obviously children will be able to practise both forehand and backhand strokes, with challenges (such as who can keep the ball going the longest) being frequently introduced to maintain enthusiasm.

Skills with a racket and ball

This particular series of suggested skills is obviously dependent on the availability of sufficient rackets, whether they are badminton, tennis, or the shorter-handled plastic rackets. The small foam ball is the most suitable ball for this type of activity; ideally it should be used with a badminton or plastic racket which are lighter than a tennis racket for the smaller or younger child to wield.

All the bat and ball practices suggested in the previous section can be used for racket work, and if ability allows the overhead serve action may be introduced. With the throwing arm at full stretch, the child releases the ball up into the air where it is struck with the racket (also at full stretch), using an overhead throwing action which begins from behind the head.

Skills with a stick and ball

As stated earlier in this chapter, if a wooden hockey or shinty stick is used indoors, it is advisable to cover the head of the stick with a sock to protect the floor surface. This procedure is not necessary if the children use a plastic or polypropylene stick.

According to availability of equipment, it is possible to use either tennis, or foam balls. The last have a tendency to be rather bouncy, while tennis balls are a little heavier to push and dribble, but possibly are the best choice for all round practising.

The skills associated with this equipment fall under the following headings: juggling, dribbling, pushing, shooting, scooping, and stopping.

(a) **Juggling** can consist of simple fun-activities such as (a) holding the stick with a hand at either end, the child attempts to climb over and bring the stick back over the head without letting go (see diagram 18, below); (b) holding the stick close to its head, the player uses it as a bat, trying to keep the ball in the air by hitting it with the stick.

juggling – climbing through the stick without letting go

batting the ball using both hands to hold the stick

batting the ball using one hand, and with the other trying to catch the ball

18 Stick and ball

(b) **Dribbling** will be a natural movement for the children to attempt when given a stick and ball, and tasks set should be varied and challenging. For instance, (a) players dribble round the room as fast as possible, until the whistle is blown, when both child and ball have to stop – the last player to stop loses a life; (b) players spell out their own names in big letters by dribbling the ball across the floor; (c) players dribble between two lines, and the first to finish, or whoever scores the most runs in a set time, is the winner; (d) as above, but players must negotiate obstacles, e.g. beanbags, hoops, skittles.

In directional dribbling, players dribble forwards and backwards, changing direction when the whistle is blown. This may also be attempted with children moving to left, right. Commands can be verbal if preferred – forward, left and right.

To encourage accuracy, lines already existing on the floor can be followed by the children when dribbling both forwards and backwards.

When working indoors, striking the ball should always be limited to a push in order to minimise the possibility of accidents.

(c) **Pushing** should be practised with the right hand holding the stick just above the head to enable a controlled forward push to propel the ball. Both distance and accuracy can be improved by setting up targets or goals and increasing the distance between them and the players.

Using a wall or a bench turned on its side, pushing can be incorporated with stopping. The rebound ball has to be stopped and controlled by the player before the push can be repeated. Competition can easily be introduced by means of speed and accuracy (e.g. from a set distance, who can be first to hit a target five times).

Dribbling can also be linked to pushing in the following ways: (a) the player pushes the ball against a wall or bench, runs after it, collects the rebound, and dribbles back to the line; (b) the player pushes the ball to a set line, runs after it, and dribbles back to the starting position, ensuring that the ball has crossed the farther line either as a result of the push, or by dribbling. All these pushing practices can also be attempted by the player kicking the ball (as in goalkeeping).

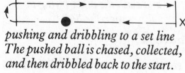

pushing and dribbling to a set line
The pushed ball is chased, collected, and then dribbled back to the start.

scooping a stationary ball over a bench

19 *Pushing and dribbling*

(d) **Scooping**, a more difficult skill, can be practised with the children working in the following ways, using a stationary ball: (a) the player scoops a ball over a line or skipping rope placed on the floor; (b) the player tries to scoop the ball over a bench; (c) the player tries to scoop the ball over a horizontal chalk line (drawn about 30 cm from the floor) on a facing wall; (d) the player scoops a ball into a container (bucket, box, or crate); (e) the player tries to scoop a ball through a hoop or a space in the wall bars.

Skills with a Rugby ball

A useful practice which can be tried with or without a ball in the hands is dodging and swerving in and out of all the other children while jogging round the hall. This footwork training can be intensified by including sudden changes of speed and/or direction (using side steps) either on verbal commands or at the blast of a whistle.

In the early stages of skills learning, throwing and catching can be practised individually by children throwing the ball up in the air and reaching out to retrieve it.

dodging and swerving when carrying a ball

throwing and catching   *pick-up*   *grub kick*

20 Rugby

Pick-ups are another important aspect of Rugby which can easily be developed in a confined space, offering several possible ways of creating competition among the children. For instance (a) which child can be the first to pick up his/her own ball and return to his place; (b) as above, but the child continues on to a second marker before returning; (c) who can be the first child to pick up the ball, run round a marker, and back to the starting place; (d) who can be the first child to pick up the ball, run round a marker, replace the ball and continue back to the starting position.

The easiest of the kicking skills which can be safely tried indoors is the grub kick, which is, basically, kicking the ball when it is on the ground. The children can try kicking a stationary ball, then progress to dribbling forward to a set marker while attempting to beat the rest of the class.

These moves can be extended to create more realistic and meaningful practices:

(a) the player drops the ball to the floor and then kicks it forward, follows it, and continues to dribble or kick the ball across the space;

(b) the dropped ball is kicked, chased, and picked up by the player who then runs round a post or marker before returning to the starting position;

(c) as (b), but instead of the player running back to the start he/she has to ground the ball he has picked up across a set line (as for a try);

(d) using mats for landing areas, a grub kick may be followed by the player falling on the ball after it has reached the safety of the mats. To ensure that the ball reaches the mats, it may be necessary for the player to dribble the ball.

3
Partner Skills and Games

Developing from individual work, children should have the opportunity to learn to cooperate with another child and also to compete against one another under varying conditions and with an assortment of equipment.

Many of the activities outlined in the previous chapter provide the foundation for partner and eventually for group work. However, it is important not to forget the basic outline of a lesson, with the need for active involvement of all the children at the beginning, gradually progressing through the necessary individual stages before attempting partner or group work.

Partner skills with a tennis or foam ball

The activities which involve the use of this type of ball are arranged under three headings: bouncing, batting, and throwing and catching.

(a) Bouncing with a partner

Standing 3 or 4 metres apart, and using both hands, children bounce the ball to one another. This exercise may then be developed to one-handed throwing and catching (using both right and left hands) with a possible increase in the distance between the two children. If a target on which the ball must bounce is introduced, the skill becomes even more difficult and challenging, particularly if a specific task is set (e.g. who can be the first to hit the target 10 times).

Standing closer together and using the hand as a bat, children pat the ball to the floor alternately. The idea of speed can be introduced (e.g. who can do 20 pats fastest) and also accuracy (by putting a mark on the floor).

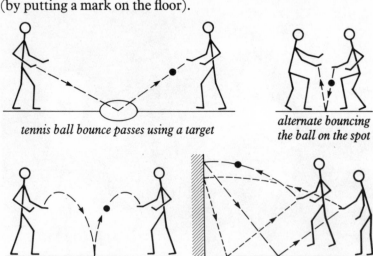

tennis ball bounce passes using a target

alternate bouncing the ball on the spot

alternate patting the ball, letting it bounce once between each hit

alternate patting and bouncing against a wall

21 *Bouncing*

These activities may be varied by getting the children to bounce the ball alternately, or after a set number of hits, or after a task has been performed: (i) one child bounces the ball right round his/her own body in both directions, then the partner repeats the action; (ii) one child bounces the ball round his/her body in a figure of eight through the legs (see page 16 and diagram 7), then the partner repeats the action; (iii) one child bounces the ball 10 times on the spot using one hand, then the partner does the same. This action is repeated using the other hand, so building up a routine of simple movements.

(b) Batting with a partner

Standing facing one another, children pat the ball into the air, using an open hand, and allow it to bounce once before it is either hit again by the same child or by the partner. This sequence is repeated and can be adapted to offer the following challenges: (i) batting the ball alternately after it has bounced once only – who can be the first pair to do this 20 times; (ii) as (i), but each child bats the ball 5 times in succession before the partner takes over; (iii) as (i) and (ii), but using the other hand; (iv) seeing how many alternate hits can be made both with and without letting the ball bounce in between each hit.

Many of these practices can be further developed with the additional use of a wall or similar surface. The ball is hit against the wall and allowed to bounce before it is returned. As with previous partner work, this task may be presented in a variety of ways, with children either batting the ball alternately, or after a set number of hits.

By creating a target area on the wall (chalk mark, hoop, window ladder spaces, or similar), the task becomes more difficult and challenging and offers wider scope for competition.

So far, the competition created by this partner work has been between couples. By introducing simple game-like activities, it is also possible to develop the spirit of competition between the individual and his/her own partner.

Using an existing line on the floor, or a mark made by a skipping rope or in chalk, two children face one another across the line and try to hit the ball over it, allowing it to bounce once between each hit. By allowing the children to make their own rules, or working on the lines of table tennis, a simple game can be developed. This can be adapted by substituting a hoop for the line and trying to hit each return so that it bounces inside the hoop, making it more difficult for the partner to return the ball.

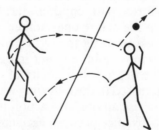

Using a line on the floor, a simple form of tennis is played.

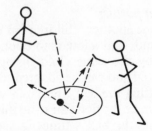

Using a hoop, partners make each hit bounce inside it, so that it is difficult for the opponent to return the ball.

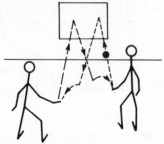

The ball must always hit the target on the wall after each bat. If either the target or the ball is missed, the opponent gains a point.

22 *Hitting games in twos*

This type of game will encourage the use of both the right and left hands. Points may be scored if the batted ball fails to bounce in the hoop or over the line, or the partner fails to return it after it has bounced once.

A simple form of hand ball may also be introduced, using a small area of the wall which the ball always has to hit after being batted alternately by the two players. It may be volleyed or allowed to bounce once, with basic rules and scoring (as in the previous activity).

(c) Throwing and catching with a partner

Standing 4 or 5 metres apart, children start by using two hands to throw and catch the ball to one another, using an underarm action, and progress to using the right hand and then the left (they may have to move a little closer initially when using the weaker hand). The degree of difficulty of this very important practice can be increased in the following ways: by (i) encouraging the children to use an overarm action for all the practices; (ii) increasing the distance between each couple; (iii) introducing a second ball, thus creating the need for improved timing and co-ordination; (iv) throwing the ball slightly to the side or above the partner who has to reach out and sometimes even move to catch the ball.

As an alternative to this type of throwing and catching, the ball may be thrown high into the air (if ceiling height allows) with the partner moving underneath the ball to catch it. Tackle this practice with both hands initially, then with the right hand alone, and finally with the left.

In games involving fielding (e.g. cricket, rounders, stoolball) children are often faced with a rolling or bouncing ball, and combined practices dealing with these aspects are also important. Pairs facing one another use any type of throw, which should land short of their partners who field the ball after one bounce. By intentionally increasing the distances by which the balls drop short, the task can be developed a stage further, as the fielder is required to move forward for the ball which is then immediately thrown back to the partner.

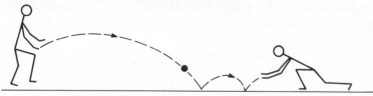

The fielder is made to move for a short throw.

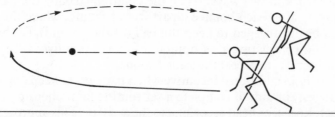

The fielder chases a rolled ball, stops it, and throws it back to a partner.

23 Fielding

A more active learning situation can be established by pairs standing side by side with one partner holding a ball which is rolled forward (not too fast) while the other child chases and tries to field it. Provided the ball is not rolled too quickly and the direction is varied slightly, children may be encouraged to overtake the ball before trying to stop it, and also to throw it accurately back to a partner faster than other pairs do.

Another approach for improving accuracy in throwing is for

partners to face one another either side of a window ladder and to try to pass the ball through the apparatus without actually touching it. This can be tried using both hands, then the right hand only, then the left, and also using an underarm and an overarm throw.

For greater involvement, the pairs can compete to discover who can pass the ball the most times within a set period, or who can be the first pair to complete 20 passes. A variation can be introduced by using a target area on the wall.

With many of the throwing and catching partner skills, the introduction of the idea of losing a life offers another alternative. Starting with the use of both hands together, whoever drops the ball is reduced to using only one hand, then drops on to one knee, then on to both knees, and eventually sits on the floor. The restrictions come into force progressively each time the ball is dropped. However if, say, three consecutive balls are caught, then a restriction is lifted, and it is possible for a child to be kneeling and then gradually to work back to standing and using both hands by catching the ball nine times in succession.

Partner skills in football

(a) Juggling

The skills covered in Chapter 2, page 19, can be modified for partner work in two ways: (i) by the children striking the ball alternately after each bounce (apart from heading, where they should be encouraged to keep the ball off the ground); (ii) by each child completing a set number of moves (say five) before the partner has to repeat the same actions.

There is an additional incentive when pairs try to keep going the longest, or aim to complete a set routine first, choosing to use feet, knees, or head according to the activity. This approach to football skills alone provides plenty to occupy most boys and girls.

(b) Passing

Standing 3 or 4 metres apart, the children use the inside first of one foot then of the other to try to pass the ball accurately to a partner. The ball should be kept on the floor with the pass being trapped (controlled) by the side or sole of the foot (both right and left). To extend this particular skill further, 'two touch passing' can be introduced (one touch to trap the ball, the second one to pass it), and the additional variation of using the same foot for both touches, or one foot to trap and the other to pass the ball, can provide an even greater challenge to the more able players, especially in a competition.

(c) Throw-in

Taking advantage of any lines already existing on the floor, the child stands behind the line with a ball and throws it to a partner who has to trap it. Once the ball is under control, the move is repeated, with the children changing roles. The practice may then be taken a stage further with the ball having to be trapped by (i) the sole of the foot; (ii) the inside of the foot or leg; (iii) the chest; and then passed back to the partner who has moved inside the line.

Two touch passing (explained above) can be introduced in this type of move, and so can heading the throw-in, providing an alternative to trapping and passing.

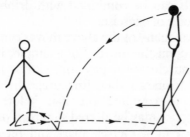

A throw-in is trapped by the partner, and passed back to the player who moves to receive it.

(d) Dribbling

As described in Chapter 2 (pages 18–19), this basic skill can be attempted in a variety of ways, using both feet or either the right or the left foot, and with the ball being touched with the inside or outside of the foot. Initially players should attempt to dribble a straight course across the room, with the ball being taken by first one and then the other partner in the course of completing the task. Progress to a more complicated route round chalk marks, skittles, or beanbags.

This individual skill can easily be combined with others to create more complex and demanding learning situations which are closely linked to those of a game.

With pairs standing 3 or 4 metres apart, the player with the ball dribbles round a partner and back to the starting point,

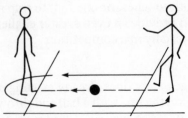

The ball is dribbled round a partner and then pushed to him/her to repeat the task.

24 Football

then passes the ball to the partner who repeats the action. Substituting a throw-in for the pass, the same routine can be varied. The whole sequence can also be attempted several times with a restriction on how the ball is dribbled (e.g. with the inside of the foot only; with the left foot only).

Juggling skills can be combined with dribbling to give an even greater choice of exercises.

If space allows, many of the above moves can be extended to children working on the move. For example, in a small circle players jog round clockwise or anticlockwise passing the ball across the circle to one another. Encourage dribbling and using different ways of trapping the ball before it is passed. This type of practice may be altered slightly if pairs move in the same direction 3 or 4 metres apart and repeat the passing procedure while crossing the area.

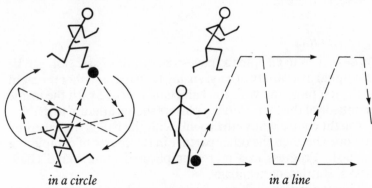

in a circle *in a line*

25 *Dribbling and passing on the move*

(e) Goalkeeping and shooting

Suitable goals can be set up using skittles, beanbags, benches turned on their sides (the ball must touch the flat side for a goal), and so on, with children taking it in turns either to shoot or keep goal for a set number of balls.

Indoors, children must be limited to controlling the ball and keeping it either on the floor or below knee height. This activity can also be attempted with the goalkeeper kneeling on a mat in front of a bench (or similar object) which has to be defended. This encourages the keeper actually to dive and get behind the ball as opposed to using just legs or hands to stop it.

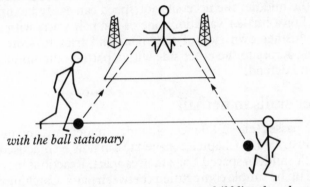

with the ball stationary

dribbling then shooting

26 Goalkeeping and shooting

To improve accuracy in shooting, pairs can practise trying to hit a skittle or a target on the wall. Progress to dribbling and shooting.

In a 1 v 1 game, children start in the centre of the room and on the whistle or verbal command try to dribble the ball away from

In each of these situations, the player is trying to dribble the ball over the opponent's line.

27 1 v 1 situations

1 v 1 situation

their partners over their own line, or to hit their own wall to score a point. With pairs starting at the edge of the room and the ball in the middle, the necessity for speed can easily be introduced. For a further variation, one of the pair starts with the ball on his/her own side of the room and tries to score by dribbling across to the other side with a partner attempting to tackle and defend.

Partner skills in netball

The five passes (chest, bounce, shoulder, underarm, and overhead) illustrated in Chapter 2 (page 21) can now be practised in twos with children spaced 3 or 4 metres apart. Reactions may be speeded up by simple competitions between pairs. Catching can be made more difficult by restricting children to the use of one hand (either right or left). Eventually, by placing the ball a couple of metres to the side of a partner it is also possible to incorporate footwork into these throwing and catching practices.

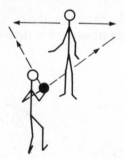

The player has to move to the left or right to receive the pass.

Progression of these skills then requires both players to move while passing (remember that only one step is permitted after catching the ball). As in soccer passing, this practice can be undertaken with players either moving in circles or travelling forwards.

For improving accuracy, passing can be attempted through wall bars or at a target on the wall with the rebound caught before it bounces. (This is similar to tennis ball partner work, page 34.)

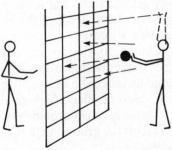

Players use the window ladder for chest, shoulder, overhead and underarm passes.

28 *Netball passing*

If adequate equipment is available, shooting practice can also involve goalkeeping, with the partners taking it in turn to shoot and then defend. Encourage both players to jump for any rebound ball which does not score.

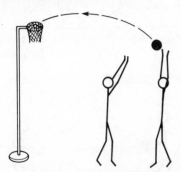

29 *Netball shooting and goalkeeping*

Dodging and marking is one concept of netball that children often find difficult to grasp. They have a tendency to follow the ball regardless of the inevitable crowding. Dodging and marking need constant practice. Partners stand one behind the other, and the back player dodges while the front one marks. To avoid having children running the length of the hall, confine movements to 2 or 3 metres to right and left, thereby forcing the dodger really to concentrate on getting free and past a suitable mark or line on the floor having escaped the marking player. Encourage change of speed and direction to achieve this.

Partner skills in volleyball

The dig and volley actions (see Chapter 2, page 22) should be practised with partners hand-feeding the ball initially. When this can be done with a degree of success, a rally should be attempted with the ball permitted to bounce once between each hit. When children have mastered this ability to maintain a rally, the ball should no longer be allowed to bounce, enabling a more realistic practice to develop. As with all the other activities, competition can easily be promoted between the pairs: e.g. who can keep the ball off the ground with the highest number of alternate digs/volleys.

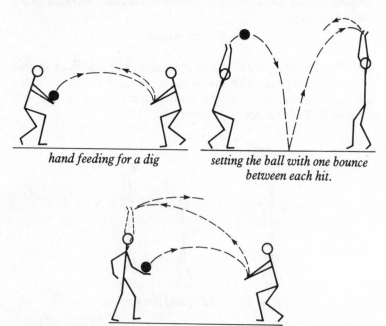

hand feeding for a dig

setting the ball with one bounce between each hit.

The ball is served and, using digging and setting, the players try to keep it off the floor.

Combining the two main ways of striking the ball extends the range of partner practices further, and with the addition of a gentle serve to put the ball in the air (replacing the throw) the main elements of the game may be learned. A net, or simply a string, hung across the middle of the hall (from high jump stands, basketball rings, or existing fitments) creates the opportunity for all the children to put their newly-acquired skills to the test. Obviously the height should vary according to the size and ability of the children (as a rough guide, get the children to stretch their arms up above their heads and take the height from that level, increasing it as ability improves).

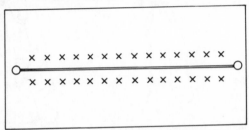

To enable all children to work with a net, a string is hung from one end of the hall to the other.

30 Volleyball

All the activities covered so far can be repeated over the net. Encourage children to give more height to the ball. Eventually a I v I game can be established with a simple scoring system operating. Each pair should have a small playing area using a net with boundaries provided by (i) existing lines on the floor; (ii) walls, both side and back; (iii) benches; (iv) chalk lines; or (v) skipping ropes.

To put the ball into play, one player throws it over the net, allowing one bounce between each hit. Initially no restriction should be imposed on the number of hits in succession permitted to one child. Points may be won if the opponent hits the ball out, under the net, or misses it. After a while, a serve can be substituted for a throw to start a rally, and if ability allows the ball should now be volleyed.

Without realising it, the more able may begin to play the ball by jumping at the net and tapping the ball down. This move, called a 'smash', can be introduced in practice form if several children are already attempting it. Height is necessary, and good jumping from a standing or moving take-off needs lots of practice. Try these incentives:

(a) partners face one another across the net and jump and touch hands above it;
(b) one player hits a ball from a partner's outstretched hands, knocking it down to the ground;

(c) one player jumps and hits down to the ground a ball thrown into the air by a partner.

This last variation can first be attempted without a net, then the ball should be thrown into the air above and close to the net (see diagram 31). *Note*: Ensure that the children are well spaced and hitting away from each other, preferably towards a wall.

jumping to touch hands above the net *jumping to hit the ball down to the floor* *jumping to hit a hand-fed ball over the net down to the floor*

31 *Practices for a smash*

Partner skills with a bat and ball

Virtually all the ideas in the tennis and foam ball batting section (pages 33–4) can easily be adapted to bat and ball work.

Small foam balls are the most suitable for this particular work; they require little effort to hit them to a partner or opponent, and more importantly, stray hits do not present a hazard to other children. However, this practice should not be completely limited to one shape bat and one kind of ball. Children should at some stage have an opportunity to try out various types of bats and balls, extending their experience and further developing hand and eye coordination.

To increase the difficult in the 1 v 1 game, a string or net can be stretched across the middle of hall (as for volleyball, described in the previous section), and a simplified game of table tennis can be played. Children serve by throwing the ball in the air, letting it bounce, and then hitting it over the net. As an alternative to a net, benches put end to end, or skipping ropes tied between rounders posts, can be used. If a large space, such as a sports hall, is available, individual nets can be set up using canes supported on skittles.

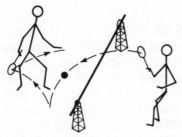

32 Batting in twos over a cane resting on skittles

Partner skills with a racket and ball or shuttlecock

Working with a wooden or plastic racket and ball or shuttle-cock, children can use all the practices and games explained under tennis and foam ball batting (pages 16–17) and bat and ball (pages 25–6) to provide progressive, challenging and often competitive situations.

As previously mentioned, a badminton racket can easily be used with a foam ball as well as with a shuttlecock, giving a variety of experience without the need for a selection of expensive rackets. Reactions and coordination are improved as children find the need to adapt to the speed of the ball or shuttle-cock as it travels through the air.

The only restriction applicable to this section is the obvious one – a shuttlecock cannot be hit against a wall for accuracy or to establish a rally with a partner.

Partner skills with a stick and ball

Working with a partner increases the range of skills that can now be practised, including pushing, dribbling, stopping, passing, shooting, scooping, kicking, tackling and bullying.

(a) Push passing

Partners are spaced 3 to 4 metres apart and try to push the ball accurately to one another. They must remember to have both hands well apart on the stick and to let it 'give' on stopping in order to reduce the possibility of the ball jumping over the stick head, or bouncing off it. Once a satisfactory level of attainment has been reached, pairs can be encouraged to beat each other by (i) completing 20 passes; (ii) scoring the highest number of passes in 30 seconds.

(b) Dribbling

Dribbling can be practised in several ways. Children should have hands well apart on the stick and keep the ball constantly in contact with the stick head, then pairs (i) play follow-my-leader, with a partner trying to shadow the leader's every movement; (ii) take it in turn to dribble a ball to a set line and back; (iii) as (ii), but dribbling the ball in and out of beanbags or similar markers. If ability allows, children can also attempt to (iv) dribble the ball backwards; (v) dribble forwards by tapping the ball alternately on the right and then the left side, turning the stick head for every hit (an Indian dribble).

reverse stick dribbling, turning the head of the stick between each tap of the ball

pathway of the ball when players use this type of dribbling

33 *Stick and ball*

Combining passing with dribbling provides a useful and progressive step in establishing the basic skills needed in a game. Initially the following practices should be tried out before any element of competition is introduced.

(i)   With pairs facing one another and spaced 3 to 4 metres apart, the player dribbles the ball round a partner and then back to the starting place before turning to push the ball across for the partner to repeat the task. Children should go to the left of the partner to ensure that they turn to the right when changing direction.

(ii) For passing on the move in twos, if space allows, players jog round in a circle (both clockwise and anticlockwise) passing across the space to one another. The ball may be dribbled a short way before being returned to a space about a metre in front of the partner.

(iii) For passing while moving, pairs, spaced apart, move in the same direction (e.g. across the hall), dribbling and passing to one another as they go. (See diagram 25, football dribbling and passing, page 38).

In passing on the move, it is important to make sure that the children experience stopping, controlling and passing a ball both on the right and on the left sides of their bodies, as the degree of difficulty is not the same. There is a need to turn both the body and the feet round to face the right when receiving a ball from that direction, or if attempting to push one to the right. Receiving or passing a ball on the left side of the body is relatively easy in comparison.

(c) Kicking

This activity is often neglected, but it is necessary if goalkeepers are to perform their team roles properly.

The pushing and stopping partner activities suggested above can be repeated kicking the ball with the inside of the foot. Developing from this movement, children can continue to kick the ball and also try to score a goal by beating a partner who has to defend the shot and stop the ball from going into a goal created by two beanbags about 2 to 3 metres apart. Each child is therefore able to practise the combined skills of shooting and defending.

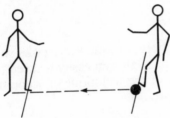

passing the ball to a partner

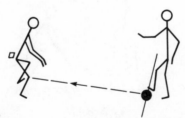

shooting against a partner who is defending a goal (this can also be tried using sticks)

34 Kicking

Variations: The idea of using small individual goals can easily be adapted to include stickwork (e.g. stopping, passing, and pushing). Instead of kicking the ball to score a goal, a push pass can be tried, with the opponent using either a stick only or feet only to stop the shot. Eventually encourage the children to stop the ball with either the stick or the feet, according to the shot and the situation.

(d) Shooting

This activity is closely linked with some of the skills covered above. As suggested under individual skills (Chapter 2, page 28), shooting can be practised with the use of a target such as a skittle, container, bench on its side, chalk mark on the wall, and so on. Working in twos, children can take turns at shooting at a target from (i) a set marker on the floor, using a stationary ball; (ii) a set marker, first having dribbled and stopped the ball.

Using improvised goals, as described in the section on Kicking, above, the two shooting practices can be combined with players taking turns at keeping goal. Points can be awarded on a simple basis: one for every goal scored by the shooter, one for every goal saved by the keeper. Allow 10 shots each, so that children can compete not only against their partners but also against all the other players who are trying to gain the maximum score.

(e) Scooping

With very little alteration, the same tasks suggested for individual work (see page 28) can easily be used for partner work, with the addition of the technique of scooping the ball over a partner's stick head.

A stationary ball is scooped over the partner's stick head.

35 *Scooping*

(f) Tackling

Introduce this activity by challenging the children to tackle and gain possession of a partner's ball. Encourage those in possession of the ball to try to dribble towards and past a partner without letting him/her get the ball away.

(g) The bully

Standing astride a line, children face one another with the ball placed between them on the line. Hands are held apart on the stick, which must first touch the ground and then the partner's stick, this move being repeated twice more before play commences.

I
Stand with feet astride the line, stick off the ground.

2
Stick touches the ground (on own side of the line).

3
The stick touches the opponent's stick in the air.

Note: *Actions 2 and 3 are repeated twice more before either player may attempt to hit the ball*

36 *The bully*

Once children master this procedure, the activity can include players dribbling the ball away and trying to reach a set line or mark to score a point. This practice can be extended further (if space allows) by introducing improvised goals or targets. Children should be encouraged to win the bully, then dribble to their goal or target and score, while the opponent tackles and tries to regain possession of the ball in an effort to score on his/her own account. In this way, a simple game of I v I is set up.

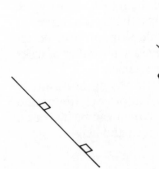  

I v I game situation with goals

Partner skills with a skipping rope

Working in twos with only one rope, pairs can attempt to skip together on the spot with the rope being swung both fowards and backwards. Initially allow a double jump to each swing of the rope, then just one jump for every rotation of the rope. Children can be given challenges such as (i) which pair can complete 20 skips first; (ii) which pair can go on skipping the longest.

More complicated footwork can be introduced (e.g. landing on alternate feet; trying to skip and travel, and so on).

in twos, using one rope

in twos, mirroring (one copies the other exactly)

jumping over a partner's rotating rope

37 *Skipping*

Using one rope each, pairs can try mirroring a partner on the spot. Whatever type of skip or swing of the rope is done by one child, the other should try to copy at exactly the same time. If ability and space allow, travelling while skipping can be included in the routine. Alternatively, give a set number of tasks and see which pair can devise the best sequence.

Jumping or even hopping over a rope swung horizontally round in a circle can also provide a way of improving timing and coordination. The difficulty of the movement can be increased if the child rotating the rope varies its speed and height.

Partner skills with quoits

With very little effort, many relevant throwing and catching activities can be organised on similar lines to those described under tennis and foam ball partner skills (see pages 34–6). Do not forget the need to use both the right and the left hand for practising these skills.

Rolling the quoit to a partner also proves quite a difficult task, requiring a certain amount of expertise. So does trying to throw the quoit so that it hooks over a partner's arm. For this activity, a point could be given for every accurate throw, with a target of, say, 5 points to aim for in a given time.

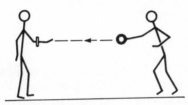

aiming a thrown quoit to hook over a partner's arm

38 Quoits

The addition of a second quoit for the players to throw and catch can also increase the element of difficulty and fun.

Partner skills with beanbags

Yet again, the range of throwing and catching activities for twos can be based upon those already outlined in detail for use with a tennis or foam ball (see pages 34–6).

Follow-my-leader, with children balancing a beanbag on the head, or gripping one between the knees, can also provide some fun. A more challenging task can be introduced by arranging obstacles round which the children have to travel, or by including a second beanbag which has to be thrown and caught while the players travel.

Partner skills with hoops

Partner work using this item of small apparatus is largely restricted to rolling activities: (a) rolling the hoop to a partner who stands about 3 to 4 metres away; (b) rolling the hoop between set lines while trying to beat a partner; (c) as (b), but negotiating obstacles (e.g. beanbags) on the floor while travelling across the space between two markers; (d) rolling a hoop through which a partner tries to climb while it is rotating (provided that hoops of sufficient diameter are available).

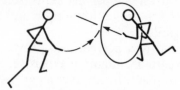

A partner runs through the hoop while it is rolling.

39 Hoops

Partner skills for cricket

The basic actions of throwing, catching and batting have been covered in some detail in the individual skills sections of Chapter 2 based on tennis and foam ball and bat and ball work. Ways of improving and developing this vital groundwork, including some techniques for fielding, have been explained earlier in this chapter (pages 34–6). As a follow-up to these practices, children can now be given the opportunity to learn the basic bowling and batting actions required for the game of cricket. (Obviously a tennis or foam ball should be substituted for a cricket ball.)

(a) Improving accuracy and fielding
(i)   Partners face one another with a floor target placed between them. One player throws to hit the target, and the ball is fielded and rolled back by the partner. Children have 10 throws each and then change over. *Note*: Always encourage players to move in, pick the ball up and throw it in one continuous movement.
(ii) As (i), but the ball is returned with a throw.
(iii) When practising a throw to hit a moving target, place a large ball between each pair of players and let children, by throwing a small ball, try to move it over the partner's line.

(b) Bowling
Having tackled these kinds of activities, children can progress to bowling to one another across the room, using a coiled position, sideways on, with the free arm pointing at the partner.

coiled position   *bounding stride*

Gradually the bounce of the ball will become more consistent, and with the introduction of a chalk target marked on the floor in front of each player the bowling can be made more challenging, with balls aimed to bounce on these targets.

The run-up may be introduced, with the bowler being encouraged to run and bound on to the same foot as the bowling arm, lifting the other leg in the air as if poised to overbalance while uncoiling the arm in preparation for releasing the ball.

Once this action has been mastered, the whole procedure should be joined together; with more able pupils a floor target can be aimed for and/or a wicket (playground stumps, chalked on a wall, or drawn on paper attached to the wall) with the partner fielding the rebound ball.

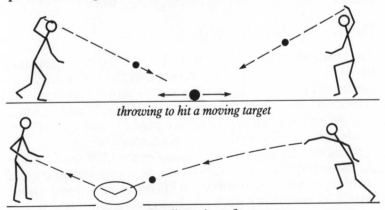

throwing to hit a moving target

overarm bowling using a floor target

40 Cricket: bowling

(c) Batting

When batting, children should be encouraged to adopt the correct stance (as shown in diagram 41) and grip right from the beginning. A backward defensive stroke can be played on a ball that a partner delivers from an underarm bowl released at hip height.

stance   backlift   defensive batting
                                              on the back foot

41 Cricket: batting

For practices of this nature it may be necessary to place the batsman on a mat to protect both floor and bat. (A plywood bat shape is more than adequate for this indoor work.)

Partner skills in basketball

The similarity of this sport to netball permits an overlap of ideas for much of the basic partner work and individual skills covering throwing, catching, passing on the move, shooting, and defending. The major difference is in footwork, and children need to practise ball dribbling (see page 21) and gradually to combine this skill with those already mentioned.

By modifying and repeating many of the ideas explained in the football and hockey sections (see pages 37–8 and 46–7), it is possible to combine dribbling with throwing using a chest, bounce, or overhead pass. These movements can also be linked to shooting, with children being encouraged to jump and then shoot while in the air.

Static practices in twos, taken from those described in the netball section above (see page 40), can include the following:
(a) chest, bounce, and overhead passing to a partner;
(b) all the passes in (a) repeated through a space in a window ladder (or similar apparatus), which demands greater accuracy and concentration from the players;
(c) shooting with a partner trying to jump and block the ball.

By adapting moving practices from football and hockey partner work a steady progression of challenging situations can be arranged, such as dribbling towards a partner, moving round him/her, and returning to the starting place, then throwing the ball across for the partner to repeat the sequence. This may be developed to allow both children to move at the same time using circle or line passing practice (provided there is sufficient space available). Eventually dribbling and passing can be combined with shooting, using any rings or baskets the children happen to be moving past or towards.

Partner skills for rounders

Much of the groundwork of rounders skills has already been covered in the sections dealing with tennis and foam ball skills and bat and ball work, e.g. (a) throwing: underarm, overarm, using two hands, using the right hand only, using the left hand only, aiming at a target or through an obstacle; (b) catching: with two hands, with one hand only, from a rebound, on the bounce, in the air above the head; (c) fielding: moving to stop a rolling ball, taking a catch which is dropping short or to either side of the player; (d) batting: with one hand on the bat, standing sideways with bat extended behind the player enabling a good swing to be taken at the ball.

The bowler steps forward on to the right foot (2) and then on to the left (3, 4) while taking the right arm back. As the left foot is put down, the right arm swings forward (5), releasing the ball at about waist height. During this last move, the body weight is transferred from the right to the left foot.

42 Rounders: bowling action (right handed)

The correct distance from the bowling to the batting square can be marked on the floor so that pairs can practise the delivery of good bowls with the bowler taking a couple of steps into his/her underarm throw.

Using a lightweight (ideally foam) ball and a rounders bat, children can take it in turn to bat and bowl (say, 10 bowls each). The player using the bat does not need to hit the ball full force, but should aim at experiencing the sideways stance and the swing of the bat, always watching the ball to ensure that bat and ball connect. (*Note:* The teacher must stress the need for care and spacing while attempting this task.)

43 Rounders: bowling and batting

Like all practice situations, competition can be introduced in several ways, creating additional enthusiasm and determination in a desire to beat a set target, or the scores of other children in the group.

Partner skills for Rugby

Partner activities for this game will generally be based on handling skills, with many of the ideas suggested under individual skills work (see pages 29–30) proving adaptable to partner work.

(a) Swerving and dodging

Swerving and dodging can be practised with one player jogging towards a partner who is blocking the way, so creating the need for a side step to swerve in order to get past. Each dodge should be left as late as possible before being put into action, in an effort to outwit the defender completely.

(b) Passing

Ball handling involving throwing and catching may be organised initially as a static activity, with children adopting a sideways and forward stance to extend their range of experience in this skill. (*Note*: This is not a realistic situation and should quickly be developed.) Passing on the move (without passing the ball forwards), using either a circle or line formation, is a more appropriate task. Make sure that the pairs have an opportunity to throw and catch the ball on both sides of the body.

(c) Ball handling

A bouncing or rolling ball always makes for difficult handling, and this often tricky manoeuvre can quite easily be recreated indoors. (i) In twos, one player rolls the ball in the general direction of a partner who moves to field it and then throws it back (say, 10 turns each); (ii) as (i), but instead of throwing the ball back the partner rolls it so that a rolling ball has to be fielded by both children in turn; (iii) one player gently throws the ball so that it bounces unpredictably for a partner to field and return either by throwing or rolling, as above.

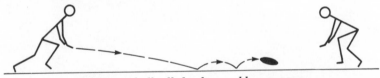

fielding a ball rolled or bounced by a partner

44 Rugby

(d) Scrum

Strength plays an important part in scrums, and the introduction to this aspect of rugby can be both challenging and enjoyable as players try to push one another backwards. Using

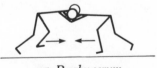

45 *Rugby scrum*

existing lines on the floor, this activity can be approached in a similar way to a tug-of-war, so that in order to win a player must push the opponent over the line. By repeating this activity when a ball has been placed between the feet of the players, the situation becomes more realistic. Players can then try to kick the ball backwards, away from their opponents' feet, at the same time that they try to push him/her forwards. If pairs are spaced out along a line, even this skill can be approached in terms of a competition, to show which half of the class proves to be the stronger, or how many times out of 10 attempts a player can beat his/her opponent. This latter variation can result in the two highest scorers being placed against one another for a grand final.

4
Small Team Games and Group Activities

The selection of team games suggested in the following pages should only be attempted after all the children have been actively involved in some form of energetic exercise, e.g. tag games. Individual or partner work taken from the relevant chapters may also provide the basis for the introductory period of an indoor lesson whatever the age of the children.

Once sufficient warm-up activities have been covered, the class may be arranged into suitable teams, preferably of three or four children at the most, to ensure that no one is inactive for any length of time.

To accommodate many small teams it is better to organise them to work across the width of the gym or hall rather than to squash them together to use the length (a common mistake made by the majority of teachers).

The term 'team game' covers a multitude of different activities, many of which can be approached in a variety of ways, both with and without using equipment.

1 The most basic approach to team games is for children to form teams behind a set line on one side of the area and to take

it in turn to travel across and back to the starting place while attempting a set task.

2 A second approach is for teams to stand behind a set line (as in 1 above) and for each child to travel across the area to a second line and wait there until all members of the team have arrived before each in turn moves back to the starting position.

3 Both these forms of relay can also be run with the addition of spaced obstacles to negotiate while the team members travel across the area.

4 A shuttle relay provides another approach (but teams must consist of even numbers if this is to work satisfactorily).

The team is equally divided, with the two groups at either side of the hall or gym facing one another across the open space. One child travels over to join the opposite team and immediately a child from that team travels back. So the process continues until all the team members have returned to their original places (that is, they have travelled in both directions across the space).

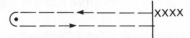

Each player in turn travels across the space, turns round a marker and comes back again (1).

Each player in turn crosses the area. Once the team members have all reached the other side, they return one at a time (2).

Shuttle relay – Number 1 crosses the area, then number 2 crosses in the opposite direction, and so on until all the players are in their starting places (4).

(a) A player completes a task by running round the team.
(b) A task is performed while travelling in and out of a team (5).

46 *Team games*

5 If the space available is restricted, then it is advisable to confine movements to avoid injury. In this situation, teams can be arranged in equally spaced lines across the area, so that the task is performed round the team members themselves, either by moving round the outside of the line, or by weaving in and out between the other children.

These five ways of organising team relays bring variety to an often limited choice of activity, and extend the range of experience offered while continuing to maintain children's interest.

Team games without equipment

All of these can be run in any of the five ways listed above.
(a) **Hopping** – children travel in one direction on the right foot and return on the left foot.
(b) **Running** – straight-forward sprinting.
(c) **Walking** – encourage children to use their arms and swing the hips from side to side.
(d) **Skipping**.
(e) **Jumping** – children keep feet together and swing the arms to gain height and length on each jump.
(f) **Crawling on hands and feet** – children travel (i) face down, forwards; (ii) face up, forwards; (iii) face up, backwards (crab walk).
(g) **Bunny hopping** – children travel from hands to feet.
(h) **Sitting** – children use the feet to (i) push the body backwards; (ii) pull the body forwards.
The following partner tasks can only be attempted if the teams are composed of even numbers and are also restricted to relay types 1, 2 and 3, above.
(a) **Piggy back** or fireman's lift for carrying a partner, with the children being matched for size (if possible). This activity can be attempted with the same child doing the carrying in both directions, or one child can carry the other across the area in one direction and they can change places for coming back.
(b) **Wheelbarrows** – this can be organised in the same two ways as described under (a) for piggy backs.
Note: Children doing the lifting hold the partner's legs above the knees; let the children walking on their hands set the pace (to avoid a dangerous stumble or collapse face forward).
(c) **Three-legged race** – use a band or spare sock to tie the inside legs of partners together.

(d) **Back to back race** – with arms linked, the pairs have to travel sideways trying to co-ordinate their leg movements.
(e) **Obstacle races** – with the teams spaced out as suggested under 5, above, players themselves form the obstacles to be negotiated.
  (i)   Leap frog – the first child runs to the back of the team and leap frogs over the other players back to the front. The second child then leap frogs over the first, runs to the back of the team and leap frogs back to his/her place; then the third, and so on until all the children have finished.
  (ii) Straddle – children crouch down low so that each member of the team in turn can straddle over the others without having to jump.
  (iii) Jumping – similar to straddle, except that children jump over the crouching team members.
  (iv) Under the legs – in turn, children crawl or slide under the legs of the team.
  (v)   Over the legs – in turn, children run and jump over the legs of the team members, who are sitting with legs stretched out and together.

(i)   *leapfrog*   (iv) *crawl*
(ii) *straddle*   (v)   *jump (over the outstretched legs)*
(iii) *jump*

47 *Team games without equipment*

Team games with equipment

The majority of the team games detailed below can be organised in the five ways explained under 1–5, above.

Tennis ball

(a) Using one hand, the player bounces the ball on the floor (possibly specify a number of bounces to be completed on a marker) and returns for the next player to repeat the task.
(b) In turn, children bat the ball, using one hand.

(c) In turn, children dribble the ball, using one or both feet.

(d) In turn, children throw the ball in the air and catch it while running, using first two hands and then just one.

(e) All the above can be incorporated with some of the juggling skills; (i) children dribble and then head the ball to catch it twice; (ii) children bounce the ball then, using the toe, flick a bounced ball in the air and catch it three times.

(f) Shuttle relay only – players throw or bounce the ball across the hall to a team member opposite before running across the area to join the back of their team line.

Quoit

(a) Children use two hands to throw and catch first one quoit and then two.

(b) The quoit is balanced on the head of a player who then travels round the team.

(c) The quoit is held between the knees of a player who then travels round the team.

(d) As in 1, 2, or 3, with each player having to complete an additional task (say, throwing and catching a set number of times, perhaps 5, before returning to the starting place).

(e) Shuttle relay – the quoit is thrown as for the tennis ball task (see (f) above).

Beanbag

This item of equipment is used in exactly the same way as the quoit in the previous section.

Hoop

(a) Children roll the hoop while travelling round the team.

(b) Children roll the hoop, then perform an additional task, such as hula-hooping, spinning, climbing through, throwing and catching, or skipping.

(c) Children skip with the hoop.

(d) Children combine skipping with one of the following activities: hula-hooping, spinning, throwing and catching, or climbing through.

Skipping rope

This item of equipment needs a certain amount of space which restricts its use to team games types 1, 2 and 4, above.

(a) Players skip while completing their turn.

(b) Each player combines skipping with an additional task – fast skipping on the spot, skipping backwards on the spot, or skipping with arms crossed – all attempted a specified number of times.

Bat and ball

(a) Using a bat, players bounce the ball on the floor.
(b) Using a bat, players hit the ball in the air, letting it bounce once between each hit.
(c) As (b), but players hit the ball without letting it bounce.
(d) All the previous tasks can be repeated with children performing an extra movement a set number of times before returning to their places, or before the next team member starts a turn – e.g. on the spot bouncing, batting.

Large ball

(a) Children bounce the ball with one hand.
(b) Players dribble the ball, using one or both feet.
(c) Players throw and catch the ball in the air.
(d) These three activities can be combined with any of the juggling skills performed a set number of times – e.g. 5 bounces on the spot, 3 headers with the ball being caught after it is headed.
(e) If a netball or basketball ring is suitably positioned, children can incorporate shooting with (i) throwing and catching in the air; (ii) bouncing. (*Note*: This activity should only be attempted as explained under team game type 1 at the beginning of this chapter.)

The shuttle relay enables even more skills to be incorporated in team games with the large ball.

(f) Throwing, using a chest, shoulder, bounce, overhead pass, or underarm pass – the player throws the ball across the area to the first person of the facing team before running to join the back of the opposite line.

Stick and ball

All the various team game formations 1–5 can be used for the following games.

(a) Dribbling races.
(b) Dribbling combined with one of the juggling skills – e.g. children climb in and out of a held stick, or hit the ball in the air with the head of the stick (similar to the skill of batting).

(c) Pushing and dribbling – the ball is pushed by the player,
chased, then dribbled to the next player either directly or
round obstacles.

Using the form of relay type 1, it is also possible to incorporate
stopping with pushing and dribbling.

(d) The player dribbles the ball across the area and then pushes
it back for the next player to stop and then dribble to repeat
the pattern of moves. Once the player has pushed the ball to
the next child, he or she then rejoins the back of the team.

(e) Using the shuttle relay formation, the players can push and
stop without dribbling the ball. The ball is pushed over to
the opposite player who stops it and pushes it back. Each
player follows the push and joins the back of the facing
team. Eventually all players complete two pushes to get
them back to their starting place.

Racket and ball
Using a tennis ball and racket, or a foam ball and a badminton or
plastic racket, children can attempt the relay races listed in the
bat and ball section (see page 64).

Braids
(a) The simple task of climbing through a braid can be turned
into an unusual and entertaining activity for children.

(b) The same task can be combined with hopping, skipping and
so on (rather than just running).

Using the single file formation (see 5, page 61), many of the
activities already described can be adapted to the three following games.

Tunnel ball
All the players stand in a line with feet apart while the equipment is rolled or slid by the first player through the tunnel of
legs. The last member of the team collects the object and races
to the front of the line while the rest of the team move back one
place. The action is repeated until the children are back in their
starting places.

(a) Teams use a large ball which is rolled by the front player.

(b) Teams use a large ball which is kicked through the tunnel of
legs by the front player and dribbled to the front by the last
player.

(c) Teams perform the same actions using a small ball.
(d) Instead of using a ball, teams slide a beanbag along the tunnel.
(e) Teams slide or roll a quoit along the tunnel.
(f) Using a hockey stick, the front player pushes a small ball through the tunnel; the last player stops it and dribbles the ball back to the front of the line using a stick.

Over the head

The object is passed backwards over the head from one team member to the next until the end of the line is reached. The last player then moves up to the front to repeat the movement.
(a) Teams use a tennis ball.
(b) Teams use a large ball.
(c) Teams use a quoit.
(d) Teams use a beanbag.

Over and under

The first player passes the object through his or her legs, and the next passes it over the head, and so on alternately to the end of the line. The last player then moves up to the front of the line to repeat the movement (always starting with a pass through the legs).

Exactly the same equipment as used for 'Over the head' can also be used for 'Over and under'.

These three games can also be tried with an additional set task, or with a varied route to be taken by the last player when moving up to the front of the line.
(i)   Players crouch down immediately the object has been passed on, so that the last player straddles or jumps over them back to the front.
(ii) The last player weaves in and out of the rest of the team on his/her way to the front.
(iii) The last player travels back alongside the team while performing a specific task – e.g. bouncing, throwing and catching, or dribbling (if the equipment is suitable).
(iv) The route suggested under (ii) can be combined with a task from (iii).

These many variations provide material suitable for a wide range of ages and abilities.

Group activities

By developing many of the skills and practices described for both individual and partner work, competitive activities and essential group work based on simplified games can easily be created.

In the following sections, a wide selection of games and skills practices for groups of three or more players are clearly explained under the headings of their associated sports.

Netball based activities

The following practices can be attempted, using all the passes previously described (chest, bounce, shoulder, overhead, and underarm).

Pepperpot

This can be tried with groups ranging from four to six children. Using one netball, the player with the ball stands 2 or 3 metres in front of the team who stand side by side facing him/her. Working from left to right, the ball is passed backwards and forwards along the line from the front player to each member of the team in turn. When the ball reaches the end of the line, the last member of the team runs with it to take the place of the front player, who joins the opposite end of the facing group. Passing continues until all players are back in their original places. (If group sizes vary, the appropriate number of additional passes can be made before the front player changes position.)

If all the groups taking part are comprised of the same number of children, this activity can be competitive, with each team trying to complete the task before the others.

Circle passing

Ideally players should be in groups of five or six for this game.

One player with the ball stands in the centre of a circle formed by the remaining players from the group. The ball is then thrown backwards and forwards between the centre player and those in the circle, working in a clockwise direction. On completion of each circle, the centre player changes places with the player who took the first pass, and passing is then repeated. When each member of the group has had a turn in the centre, the activity is completed. (See diagram 93, page 119.)

As in 'Pepperpot', groups can compete against one another, with additional passes being made if group sizes vary.

Line passing

Groups of even numbers are needed for this practice, which incorporates passing and running.

The group is divided equally, with two lines of players standing one behind the other and facing across a space of about 3 to 5 metres (according to ability). The ball is thrown from the first player in one line across to the front player of the facing line. Immediately the ball is released the player follows it across the space and joins the back of the opposite group. Eventually all the children change sides and the activity is repeated until they return to their original places.

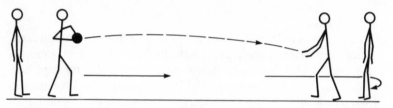

After throwing the ball, the player runs and joins the back of the opposite line.

48 .Line passing

Children taking part in this practice may need reminding that the ball is thrown before they run across to join the line opposite. The order is catch, throw, run.

A variation, which is an activity similar to 'Pepperpot', can be tried with groups of four to six children. It uses only chest, shoulder and overhead passes.

One player with the ball faces the remaining players who stand in single file. The ball is thrown to the first child and returned. This player then squats down out of the way as the ball is passed to the second player who in turn squats down as soon as the ball has been returned to the player out in front. This sequence continues until the ball reaches the last (back) player who keeps hold of it and runs to face the group, while the original facing player takes up a new position at the head of the line. Players stand up, the passing is then repeated, and the game concludes when all children are back in their starting places.

Practices in threes

(a) Provided sufficient space is available, children can practise passing on the move by forming a straight line and working across the indoor area, remembering to observe the foot-work rule on receiving the ball.

(b) Piggy-in-the-middle, or 2 v 1 – one player in the middle tries to intercept the passes of the other two children. On gaining possession of the ball, the 'piggy-in-the-middle' changes places with the player who threw the intercepted pass. The 'piggy' can either mark one player all the time, or, if quick, mark the player who is dodging to receive. Variations can be introduced by restricting the types of passes to be used.

(c) Throw-in – using existing or improvised lines, a player with the ball stands with feet up to the line and takes a throw-in. The second player marks the first at the line while the remaining player, using a space, tries to catch the throw-in. After several attempts, children change round to give each one the opportunity to experience working in the different positions.

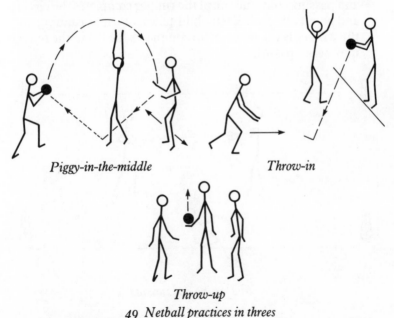

Piggy-in-the-middle   *Throw-in*

Throw-up

49 Netball practices in threes

Children should try the different types of pass to discover which is the most useful in this situation. For a more realistic practice, the person marking can give the com-

mand, 'Play!' (as given by the umpire in a game), whereup-
on the throw-in must be taken within the three seconds
allowed.

An additional variation can be created if the second player
moves to mark the dodging player on court (as opposed to
the player actually taking the throw-in).

(d) Throw-up – two players stand facing one another, arms at
sides, and about a metre apart. The third player holds the
ball in one hand at chest height, and, standing between the
two, tosses it in the air no higher than the heads of the two
players. Children change places after several goes. By introducing a simple scoring system of one point for each
throw-up won, a competition can be organised among
groups in the class.

(e) Passing and running – two players, using a specific throw set
by the teacher, try to establish a high number of passes while
the third player runs round a set course marked by skittles,
chalk marks, beanbags, or existing lines on the floor. On the
command 'Go!' passing and running start simultaneously,
and passing continues until the runner completes the circuit
and shouts 'Stop!'. Each child takes a turn at running and
the winner is the player who completes the lap in the fewest
number of passes.

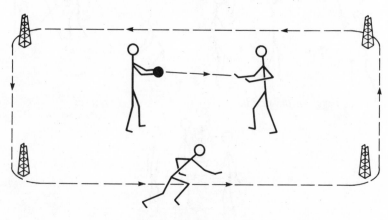

50 Passing and running

(f) Passing and running in competition – this activity can be
adapted for team competition. Working in the same way as
described in (e), three players pass the ball while three
others form a line and run round a set course to complete a

lap. Then the two groups change places and repeat the action, with all five types of pass being used in turn.

A variation can be made in this basic passing and running activity. Two groups of four to six children work in the same way as described in (f), one running in a line round a set course while the opposing group tries to complete as many passes as possible. But now the passing can include tunnel ball, over the head, or over and under sequences, as described on pages 65–6.

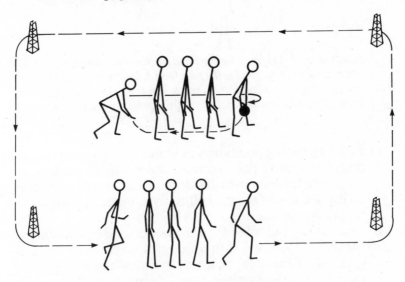

51 Teams passing and running

Practices and games for four to six players

(a) **Pivoting and passing** – children line up one behind the other except for one player who, standing forward and to the side, will act as a feeder (see diagram 52). The player at the head of the line throws the ball to the feeder who catches and directs the return pass to a point towards which the first player is running to receive it. The first player catches the pass, pivots 180° on the landing foot to face the line of players, and throws the ball to the second player before completing the 360° turn and running on to form a new line on the opposite side of the area. The activity is repeated until all the children have crossed the area, when the last in line becomes the new feeder.

(b) **2 v 2** – children have their own partner to mark and dodge.

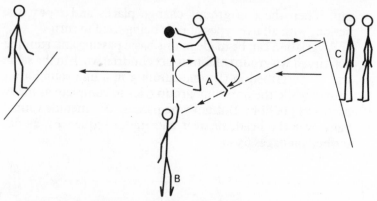

A throws the ball to B, runs forward and catches the return from B.
A pivots to face C who catches the pass from A who then moves to join
the new line opposite. C repeats the whole move. The last player pivots
through 360° and throws the ball to the front person of the new line.

52 Pivotting and passing

(c) **2 v 2** – as (b), but points may be scored if one pair completes three consecutive passes without the ball being dropped or intercepted. (Bounce passes do not count as a drop.) After each point is scored, the ball is given to the opposition to restart the passing.

(d) **2 v 2** – as (b), but using a specific area created by chalk lines, benches, or similar, with a throw-in taken when the ball goes out of the area. Scoring can follow the pattern suggested in (c). As a variation, passing can be combined with shooting (bouncing the ball in the team's own hoop, knocking over a skittle, and so on).

(e) **3 v 3** – with players being given specific tasks (shooter, centre, goalkeeper), a simple game of skittle ball can be played. The centres take it in turns to have the ball after each goal is scored, and only the goalkeeper can defend and only the shooter score. (To score, the shooter must hit a skittle placed in a hoop or a chalk circle, which cannot be entered by any player, or simply bounce the ball in the scoring area.)

(f) **4 v 4** – as (e), but with an extra centre court player.

(g) Both (e) and (f) can be played with teams having to pass the ball three times without dropping it before the shooter can attempt to score. If the ball is thrown or knocked out of the area of play, a throw-in is taken by the opposing team.

Note: The five passes can be used in all the above activities.

Hockey based activities

Many of the practices already outlined under team relays and netball activities are suitable for stick and ball work, substituting a push pass for a throw.

Practices in threes

(a) **Passing on the move** – children incorporate dribbling, stopping and push passing into this practice.
(b) **Piggy-in-the-middle**, or 2 v 1 – the 'piggy' must always keep at least a metre from the player with the ball.
(c) **Push-in** – using an existing mark on the floor, the first player pushes the ball straight along or down the line to the second player. The third player marks the second and tries to stop the ball.
(d) **Passing and running** – one player dribbles a ball round a set course while the other two players pass another ball to one another as many times as possible before the run is completed.

All these activities correspond to similar ones in the netball section above (see also netball diagrams 49 and 50).

Practices and games for four to six players

(a) **Circle passing** – groups use a push pass. (See under *Netball*, page 67.)
(b) **Pepperpot** – groups use a push pass. (See under *Netball*, page 67.)
(c) **Line passing** – in turn, children push pass the ball across to a player opposite who stops it and pushes it back. Once the ball is passed the player follows it across the space to join the back of the line opposite. This activity can also be tried with players dribbling the ball across as they change sides. (See under *Netball*, page 68.)
(d) **3 v 1** – three players try to pass the ball round a triangle before the fourth player can intercept the ball.
(e) **2 v 2** – from a bully or push pass, one team must make three consecutive passes to score a point. The game is restarted after each successful attempt by a bully or push pass to the pair conceding the point.
(f) **3 v 1** – three players try to pass the ball and hit a target defended by the fourth player.
(g) **2 v 2** – as (e), with the addition of a skittle to hit for scoring. Alternatively, a wall target can be used.

(h) **3 v 3** – players take it in turn to play goalkeeper, defence and forward, changing after each goal scored. The goal area can be created from skittles, beanbags, a bench on its side, and so on. The area of play can also be restricted by suitable boundaries so that push-ins can be included to establish a more realistic small game situation. (*Note*: Goalkeepers can use their feet to stop the ball.)

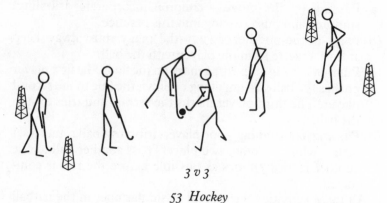

3 v 3

53 Hockey

(i) **4 v 4** – this can be played as (g) with an additional forward, or with two defences and two forwards instead of a goalkeeper.

(j) **Snakes and ladders** – players, each with a ball, line up in single file about a metre apart. The last player dribbles in and out of the line up to the front, then stops the ball. Immediately the player who is now last in the line starts to dribble in and out up to the front, and so the line gradually moves forward across the area until the target line is reached. This activity lends itself to team competition.

The line gradually moves forward as the back player dribbles in and out of the team to a new position in front. Once the back player has reached the front, the new back player follows the same route.

54 Snakes and ladders

(k) **Players, each with a ball, form a circle.** Opposite players start to dribble in and out of the remaining players, travelling in the same direction round the circle, trying to catch one another or to reach their original places first.

Opposite children dribble in and out of the circle of players, trying to beat their opponent in getting back to the starting place first.

55 Circle dribbling

Football based activities

Dribbling, passing, heading, tackling and throw-ins can all be practised using the following group activities (many of which are similar to those already explained in the netball section).

Practices in threes
(a) **Passing on the move.**
(b) **Piggy-in-the-middle,** or 2 v 1 – the 'piggy' must always keep at least a metre from the player with the ball.
(c) **Throw-in.**
(d) **Passing and running.**

Practices and games for four to six players
(a) **Pepperpot** – players head the thrown ball back to the front player.
(b) **Pepperpot (2)** – the ball is kicked backwards and forwards between the player out in front and the facing line.
(c) **Circle passing** – this can be tried with players combining the two skills of kicking and heading, as in (a) and (b).
(d) **Line passing** – each player in turn dribbles or kicks the ball across to the player opposite who repeats the movement back.

(e) **3 v 1** – when passed around a triangle, the ball has to be intercepted by the fourth player without tackling.

(f) **3 v 1 (2)** – three players try to pass the ball and hit a target defended by the fourth player.

(g) **2 v 2** – make a set number of consecutive passes to score.

(h) **2 v 2** – score by hitting a skittle.

(i) **3 v 3** – the three players are goalkeepers, defence, and forward.

(j) **4 v 4** – the four players are goalkeepers, defence, and two forwards.

(k) **Snakes and ladders**.

(l) **Circle dribbling**.

For information about activities (e)–(l), see the previous section on hockey (pages 73–5).

A lightweight or large foam ball is most suitable for this type of indoor work. Remember to restrict the flight of the ball to waist height in a game situation.

Rugby based activities

Activities and small games based on this sport will obviously be restricted to dribbling and handling skills when working indoors.

Practices in threes

(a) **Passing on the move** (always passing back).

(b) **Piggy-in-the-middle**, or 2 v 1.

(c) **Passing and running** – the player who is running carries a ball with both hands and has to place it on the floor on completion of the run; the other two pass a second ball.

(d) **Passing** – count how many passes can be made in a set time.

(e) **Line out** – one player throws the ball, the second player jumps and tips the ball into the hands of the third player. *(See diagram 56 opposite.)*

Practices and games for four to six players

(a) **Pepperpot** – throwing the ball.

(b) **Circle passing** – throwing the ball.

(c) **Line passing** – (i) the ball is thrown across the area to the opposite player who then throws it back; after throwing, the first player runs across the space to join the back of the opposite line. (ii) The first player carries the ball across the space, passing to the player opposite, who then repeats the movement back, so that players change sides.

(d) **3 v 1** – three players try to complete a set number of passes; the fourth player tries to intercept a pass.

(e) **2 v 2** – try to pass and ground the ball across the opponent's line for a point.

If the player with the ball is touched with both hands by an opponent, he/she stops and the ball must be passed backwards.

(f) **3 v 3** – as (e); no passing forwards – the ball is given to the opposition if this happens.

(g) **Snakes and ladders** – each player in turn weaves in and out of the rest of the team while carrying the ball. (See (k), page 76.)

(h) **Circle formation** – players opposite one another in the circle run clockwise dodging in and out of the remaining players while carrying a ball. (See (l), page 76.)

If ability allows, the last two practices (g) and (h), can be tried dribbling the ball instead of carrying it.

(i) **Line-outs** – one player throws the ball to a line of players who jump and try to tip it to a supporting player standing to one side.

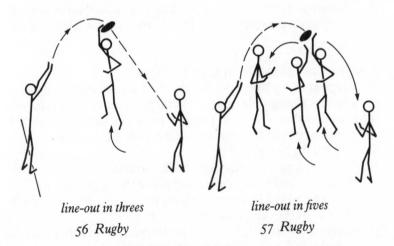

line-out in threes

56 Rugby

line-out in fives

57 Rugby

This activity can be developed by having a supporting player on either side, with those in the line-out comprising players from two opposing teams each trying to pass the ball to their own side. (After several attempts, children should change position.)

(j) **Scrum** – teams try to push their opponents backwards over a line to score. This can also be attempted with a ball placed in the scrum and players trying to drive forwards while heeling the ball backwards out of the scrum.

Basketball based activities

Much of the material suitable for basketball group practices and games is a variation of tasks previously described in both the netball and football sections (pages 67–72 and 75–6).

Practices in threes
(a) **Piggy-in-the-middle**, or 2 v 1.
(b) **Passing and dribbling** (bouncing the ball using one hand) while moving across the area.
(c) **Toss-up**, as used to start the game – one player throws the ball in the air for the other two players to jump for.
(d) **Passing and running** – two players, using a specific pass, try to establish a high number of passes while the third player dribbles (bounces) the ball round a set course. Each player takes a turn at this activity to see who can complete the course in the least number of passes.
(e) **Shooting** (subject to the availability of basketball or netball rings) – two players in turn dribble and shoot while the third defends.

Practices and games for four to six players
(a) **Pepperpot** – players use a chest, bounce, or overhead pass.
(b) **Circle passing** – players use the three passes as for (a) above.
(c) **Line passing** – in turn, players throw the ball across to the player opposite and run to join the end of the opposite line. (Use all three passes.)
(d) **Line passing** – use the same basic formation as (c), but with the player dribbling the ball across to the opposite side.
(e) **Snakes and ladders** – each player in turn dribbles the ball in and out of the rest. (See (k), page 76.)
(f) **Circle dribbling** – players opposite one another in the circle dribble the ball clockwise in and out of the remaining players. (See (l), page 76.)
(g) **2 v 2** – pairs try to establish a set number of consecutive passes to score (e.g. 5 passes without being intercepted).
(h) **2 v 2** – using a small area with established boundaries, pairs try to pass and dribble the ball to their own end and then

score. (Scoring may be by bouncing the ball in a hoop, hitting a skittle or wall target, or shooting into a ring if sufficient rings are available.)

(i) **3 v 3** – this game can be played in a similar way to (h), but with a different form of scoring. The third player stands on a bench or chair at the end of the court and has to catch the ball for his or her own team to score. Once a player scores, both the catchers change places with another player in their team, until all have had a turn at catching.

As a variation, the player on the bench (chair) holds a small hoop above his (her) head through which the ball has to be thrown to score.

3 v 3 – one player stands on a bench holding a hoop through which the ball has to be thrown to score.

58 Basketball

(j) **3 v 3** – teams score by shooting into a ring, or hitting a target placed at an appropriate height on the wall.

Volleyball based activities

A net or rope strung lengthwise down the middle of the indoor area (as described in Chapter 3, pages 42–3) is ideal for practices and small games.

Practices in threes

(a) **Digging** – standing in a triangle, players try to maintain a rally, with each player in turn digging the ball (allow one bounce between each hit). Once the children have acquired sufficient skill, this can be attempted without allowing the ball to touch the floor.

(b) **Volleying** – this should be approached in exactly the same way as digging, with the ball initially being allowed to bounce before the player volleys it.

(c) **Dig and volley** – one player with the ball throws it for the second player to dig. The ball is then volleyed by the third player for the first (the feeder) to catch. This activity is best attempted in triangular formation. Remember to change the direction in which the ball is travelling, and the tasks, after players have had several turns.

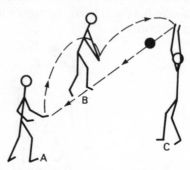

A throws the ball for B to dig to C. C then volleys for A to catch.

59 *Volleyball: practices in threes — dig and volley*

(d) As (c), but the player volleying the ball tries to do this over the net or rope.

(e) **Smash** – one player stands at the net and throws the ball into the air, above net height but close to it. Taking it in turns, the other two players run forward and jump to try with an open hand to hit the ball down to the floor on the other side of the net.

(f) **Smash and block** – the block can be practised along with the smash (explained in (e), above). The second player jumps to smash the ball when it is above net height, and the third player, positioned on the far side of the net, jumps a split second later putting up the arms in an attempt to block the ball. Timing is very important for both of these skills, and it may be necessary to lower the net or rope slightly to enable the children to experience success in this quite difficult task. *(See diagram 60 opposite.)*

(g) **Set and smash** – one player with the ball stands 5 or 6 metres away from the other two players who stand at the net about 3 metres apart. Initially the ball is thrown from the first player (furthest from the net) to the second (who is at

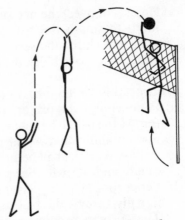

60 Volleyball: smash and block   *61 Volleyball: set and smash*

the net) who sets it high for the third player to jump for and smash over. When the children have played in all three positions, the ball can be gently served by the first player instead of being thrown.

(h) **Serve-dig-volley** – one player stands at the back of the improvised court and serves over the net to the other two players. Whoever receives the serve digs it to the net so that the third player can run forward and try to volley it over. (If the serving proves too erratic, the ball can be thrown.) Again, the children should be given an opportunity to play in all three positions.

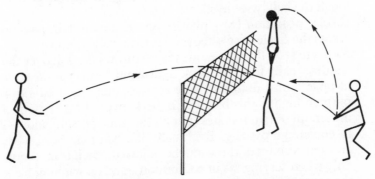

62 Volleyball: serve, dig and volley

(i) **Serve-dig-set-smash** – if ability allows, players can develop the previous task (h) to include a smash. The second player receives the serve and digs it to the third player who sets it along (not over) the net for the second player to run in and jump to smash the ball over. Provided the players have sufficient skills, the server may then be encouraged to try either to jump to block the smash or to retrieve it with a dig.

Practices and games for four to six players

(a) **Pepperpot** – the player standing out in front of the team throws the ball to be volleyed back by the rest of the group in turn. If ability allows, the team can eventually perform the activity with the ball being continuously volleyed instead of caught and thrown. (See page 67.)

(b) **Pepperpot** (2) – the player standing out in front of the team initially throws the ball for the other players to dig back. Then players progress to using a dig all the time (allowing one bounce between each pass). Eventually players volley the ball backwards and forwards without a bounce.

(c) **Circle passing** – this can be introduced with players using first the volley and then the dig action. (See page 67.)

(d) **Volleying in a circle** – standing in a circle, the players volley the ball backwards over their heads from one to another. Each series of hits (passes) is counted to see if the team can beat other teams, or which team can be the first to reach a target of 20 hits.

(e) **Circle formation** – players pass the ball at random across the circle using a dig, with each group trying to establish a high number of consecutive passes. Initially the ball may be allowed to bounce between each pass, but no player may touch the ball twice in succession.

(f) **Circle formation** (2) – players repeat the random passing across the circle of (e), above, but use a volley action.

(g) **2 v 2** – to start the game, one player throws the ball over the net diagonally from the back right-hand corner (in the style of table tennis doubles). The receiver must then pass to a partner before the ball is hit back over the net with a minimum of two touches (not by the same person) allowed to encourage passing. Eventually the ball may be served, and a maximum of three touches allowed. Each team scores only when serving (as in badminton), and on winning back the serve the two players in the serving team change places so that the second player can serve.

As with many of the previous practices, this small game situation can be played with the ball being allowed to bounce once between each hit. However, as players become

gradually more proficient, this rule can be dispensed with.
(h) **3 v 3** – using a slightly larger improvised court, the game can
be developed stage by stage as in 2 v 2 in (g), above.

Additionally, players can now attempt to dig, set and
smash when receiving a serve (as explained in practices in
threes). As an alternative, two players together may jump to
block a smash, with the third player standing ready to
retrieve the ball if it comes over.

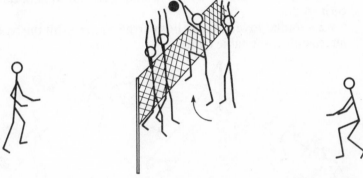

*Two players block the attempted smash, while the third player covers in
case the ball goes over. This situation is created by the dig, set and
smash routine being practised on any deep serve or return.*

63 Volleyball: 3 v 3

Bat and ball based activities

Individual nets created by a cane supported on two skittles, or a
skipping rope tied between two rounders posts, are required for
the majority of the following games and activities. However, if
the space available is limited, one net or rope hung lengthwise
(as for volleyball) at about waist height will be sufficient.

Practices and games for four players
(a) **Pepperpot** – players bat the ball underarm, with one bounce
allowed between each hit. (See page 67.)
(b) **Circle passing** – again, players bat the ball using an underarm action, allowing one bounce between each hit. (See
page 67.)
(c) **Snakes and ladders** – in turn, each player bounces the ball
on the bat while moving in and out of the line up to the front.
(d) **Line passing** – players stand in twos, facing one another
either side of a net. The ball is hit over the net to the player

opposite who returns it after only one bounce. When the first player has hit the ball, he or she runs round behind the partner who plays the return shot. In this way a rally is established with children making alternate hits.

(e) **2 v 2** – using individual improvised nets, or a section of one long net, players serve from the back right-hand corner diagonally across the court (as in table tennis doubles). To serve, the player bounces the ball which is then hit over the net using an underarm action. A simple scoring system can be introduced.

(f) **2 v 2** – similar to (e), above, but partners have to hit the ball alternately (as in table tennis).

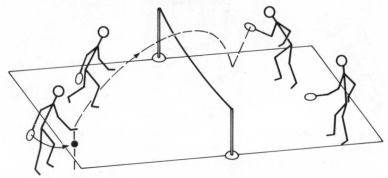

2 v 2 – serving diagonally from the back right hand corner (as for table tennis), players hit the ball alternately.

64 Bat and ball

Practices for six or more players
(a) **Circle formation** – two players, each with a bat and a ball, start from opposite sides of the circle and travel round it in the same direction running in and out between the remaining children while batting the ball in the air. The first back to his or her own place wins a point.

(b) **Line passing** – players make two equal lines facing one another across the net. The ball is served by the first player and the children take it in turn to hit it back over the net. Once a player has returned the shot, he or she moves quickly to the back of the line. The aim is to establish a continuous rally, counting the number of times the ball is played.

(c) **Players form two lines** (as for (b), above), but after playing the ball they run round the side of the net and join the back of the opposite line instead of their own.

Once the player returns the hit, he or she runs to the back of either his/her own line, or (b) the line on the other side of the net.

65 *Continuous rally*

Both group activities (b) and (c) can be used with large groups of children, and competition between groups can be encouraged by setting a target figure for continuous rally. For individual competition, a life can be lost when the player fails to hit or to return the ball. If all players start with three lives, then those who lose all three must sit out. (*Note*: A tennis ball or small foam ball is most suited to this type of activity.)

Racket and ball or shuttlecock based activities

All the practices and game situations described under bat and ball activities are also suitable for racket work, either with a small foam ball, tennis ball, or shuttlecock.

As previously mentioned, a badminton racket can be used with both a shuttlecock and a small foam ball. Thus children are enabled to experience work on both tennis and badminton skills in a confined space with the same racket. The shorter handled plastic racket is a useful alternative for the younger or smaller child.

Improvised playing areas can be created and nets set up in one of the ways already suggested. For practices and games based on badminton, the net should be placed at a height of 1.5 metres.

Only a ball should be used with the racket for activities involving hitting in the air while travelling in and out of the rest of the group; a shuttlecock used in this way is often erratic and very difficult to control.

If a doubles game is being attempted, the correct serve action can be introduced (for tennis this will be governed by the space available and by the availability of foam balls). If the playing area is restricted, an underarm serve may have to be used for ball work, with children initially adopting a table tennis type of scoring and serving system. The game can then develop to include serving the ball from both sides of the court, with four points needed for a win (as in tennis).

In a 2 v 2 game using a shuttlecock, points can only be won when a player is serving. Provided that players show an understanding of badminton, the correct serving procedure can gradually be introduced. (Both players take a turn at serving using either side of the court, and only score when serving.)

Cricket based activities

Group practices based on this sport fall into two main categories: fielding and batting. For the majority of the indoor activities which follow, it is advisable to use a tennis ball, or even an airflow or foam ball, when batting. However, a rounders or cricket ball can be used for basic throwing and catching skills with the more able pupils (subject to safety precautions).

Practices in fours

Fielding
(a) **Passing**– standing in a square and using an underarm throwing action, children practise passing the ball round the square to see which four can complete 20 passes before other groups. See how many times the ball can be thrown round the group in 30 seconds.
(b) **Passing (2)** – as (a), above, but using an overarm throw if sufficient space is available for the groups to spread out without risk of injury.
(c) **Rolling** – using the same square formation as described under (a), each player in turn rolls the ball for the next player to field and roll for the next person. (Encourage children to get down behind the ball with both hands forming a large cradle to trap it.)

(d) **Random passing** – all the skills in (a), (b) and (c) can be developed if children pass at random, either diagonally across the square or to the right or left, creating the need for players to concentrate and to react quickly.

(e) **Attacking fielding** – one player with the ball stands facing the other three who stand in single file. The player with the ball rolls it towards the first in the line, who runs forward to meet the ball, picks it up, and throws it back to the person who rolled it. Once the ball has been fielded, the fielder rejoins the back of the line so that all three players can complete the pick up. Then all move on one place, to ensure that everyone has a turn at rolling and fielding the ball.

(f) **Chasing and fielding** – one player with the ball stands alongside the other three and rolls the ball forward (away from the group). It is chased, fielded, and thrown back by each member of the group in turn. All change places so that each player both rolls and fields the ball.

A chases, fields, and then throws the ball back to B before rejoining the back of the line. B then rolls the ball again for C to field.

66 Cricket: chasing and fielding

(g) **Bowling** – using playground stumps, skittles, floor or wall targets, three of the members of the group take turns at bowling while the fourth retrieves the ball. After six bowls, the fielder changes places with one of the bowlers.

(h) **Bowling and wicket keeping** – two of the members of the

67 Bowling and wicket-keeping

group bowl in turn at a standing wicket or floor target, the third is positioned 1 or 2 metres behind this as wicket keeper, and the fourth fields any stray or missed balls. After facing six bowls, the wicket keeper and fielder change places with the two bowlers, and the practice is repeated. Each group member should practise bowling, wicket keeping and fielding.

Batting

A bat shape is adequate for indoor work with lightweight balls. Remember that it may be necessary to work on mats to protect the floor surface under certain conditions.

(a) **Batting** – using a wall target, skittle, or playground stumps for a wicket, two players standing 3 or 4 metres away take turns to feed the ball to a batsman (using an underarm throw). The batsman tries to play the ball forward back to the bowler; the fourth player fields any erratic returns. After six bowls, the group members move round (as in the fielding activities above). (*Note*: Obviously this method restricts the way the batsman has to play the ball, but it provides the player with an opportunity to get the feel of a bat and improves hand-eye co-ordination.)

(b) **Batting to the off side** – with players organised in the same way as in (a), the ball is fed (still underarm) to the 'off' side. The batsman tries to hit it to that side, with the fielder covering the strokes. As variations, (i) the ball is fed to the 'leg' side, and the batsman tries to hit to that side; (ii) two fielders (one either side), one batsman and one bowler use a wall wicket, with the ball being bowled to the off or leg side, or straight – the batsman has to react quickly and hit the ball correctly.

Throughout any batting practices, children need constant reminders about correct grip and stance. This is more important than hard hitting which should not be encouraged indoors where several groups are involved in similar activities.

If a large space is available, groups of six children can participate in a simple game, using a lightweight ball. The players are numbered 1 to 6, with 1 bowling, 2 batting, 3 wicket keeping, 4 fielding at slip, 5 fielding on the off side, and 6 fielding on the leg side. Use playground stumps or skittles as a wicket. The bowler delivers 6 bowls (an over) and then the members of the group move round one place. Initially the

The ball can be bowled to both the leg and the off side.
68 *Bowling and batting*

bowling can be underarm, and gradually developed to a standing overarm coiled action, finally progressing to a running
stride delivery if ability and space allow. Runs can be scored in
the usual way, with the addition of a 'boundary' for hitting the
opposite wall. The batsman can be caught, bowled, or stumped
out at the wicket to which he or she is running. Each batsman's
score is the difference between the runs scored and the number
of dismissals.

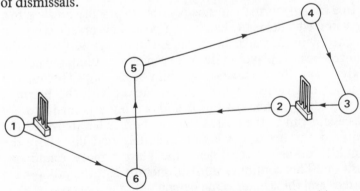

*After an over has been bowled, players move on one position, as
illustrated.*

1 Bowler	*3 Wicket-keeper*	*5 Off-side fielder*
2 Batsman	*4 Slip fielder*	*6 Leg-side fielder*

69 *Rotation game for six players*

Rounders based activities

Taking into consideration the obvious bowling and batting differences between rounders and cricket, most of the activities described for group work in cricket (above) are also suitable for improving rounders skills (with slight modifications).

In order to prevent damage or injury, a lightweight ball (foam, airflow, or tennis) must be used for all the batting activities. However, a rounders ball can safely be used for some of the fielding activities with the more able children.

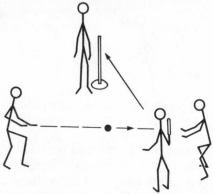

The batsman scores by reaching the post without being caught or stumped. After a set number of bowls, all the players move round.

70 Rounders: fielding and batting in fours

In a triangle formation, it is possible to practise bowling to a backstop who fields the ball to first post. This practice can also be tried with the batsman trying to run to first post before the ball reaches the player there, who can either stump the post or body stump the batsman to get him or her out. This type of practice can easily be made competitive, with the batsman having a set number of bowls and scoring a point for every successful run to the post. Once the bowler has delivered the required number of bowls (not including no-balls, above the shoulder or below the knee), the players move round one position. This continues until all members of the group have batted, and the winner is the person with the most points after the number of times caught or stumped out has been deducted.

5
Large Team Games

In this chapter, a wide variety of games suitable for classes of both single and mixed sex groups are described. They offer a choice of both activity and type of equipment used.

However, it is important to remember that, owing to the large numbers involved in this type of game situation, the children will no longer be constantly active. Therefore it is vital that some preliminary individual, partner, and even group work is covered before children are organised for any of the following games.

With the help of the skills and practices set out in earlier chapters, a structured lesson dealing with a specific sport can be quickly and easily planned. This will provide a useful learning situation which progresses from the basic individual skills through to a game situation.

In order to gain the maximum area for activity for large numbers of children, some of the games can be arranged across the width of the space available. In this way, two or even three games can be played simultaneously.

Netball based activities

1 **Captain Ball** – this game can be played with two teams of 6–10 children. Two benches (one for each team) at either end of the playing area and one netball or lightweight ball are the only items of equipment required. Half the players from each team stand on their own bench while the remaining half stay on the 'court' to play one another. The game follows the basic rules of netball, with play commencing from a centre pass and players marking an opponent. To score, the ball is passed three consecutive times amongst players of the same team without being dropped, and only then can a goal be attempted by throwing the ball to a member of the team on the bench. If the ball is caught by a member of the same team, a goal is scored, and the players on the 'court' change places with those standing on the bench. The game then restarts with a centre pass (taken alternately between teams).

For any attempt at a goal that is dropped or missed, and for any ball that goes 'off' (that is, out of the playing area), a throw-in is taken by the other team. A variation can be made: instead of the teams changing places when goals are scored, they only do so on the command 'Change!' given periodically by the teacher. Immediately the command is given, all the children actually playing leave the ball wherever it is and change places with the players on their own benches. Whoever is quickest off the bench gains possession of the ball for his or her own side and play continues from this point in the same way as above.

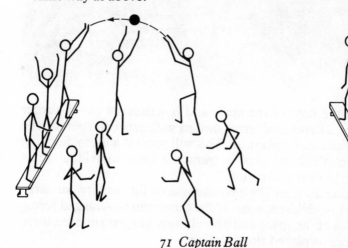

71 *Captain Ball*

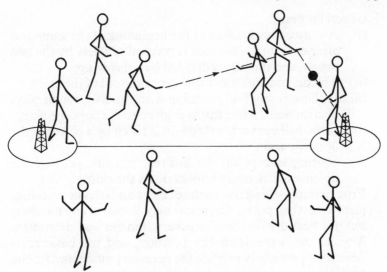

72 Skittle ball

2 **Skittle ball** – the basic aim of this game is to hit or knock down the opposing team's skittle. This can be attempted in various ways.

(a) A skittle is placed at either end of and outside the improvised playing area. One or two children are allowed to shoot and the same number allowed to defend. Players are paired off with an opponent, and shots at the target can be made from any position inside the court.

(b) As above, but by dividing the playing area either length-wise or widthwise, children can be restricted to one area only to encourage spacing.

(c) Both the games (a) and (b) can be developed further by introducing the need to make a minimum of three consecutive passes before shooting at the skittle.

(d) The skittle can be positioned inside a large hoop on the court, with players being able to move all round the hoop but not inside it. This game can be played using as variations the suggestions made in (a), (b) and (c).

(e) At either end of the playing area, mark a circle of approximately 2 metres diameter. The skittle and a defender are positioned inside this circle (only they are allowed inside it). Then the game can be played in any of the ways already outlined.

General notes:

(i)   A centre pass is taken at the beginning of the game and after each goal – the pass is taken alternately by the two teams, and initially is decided by a throw-up.

(ii)   The defender of the skittle can come out of the circle.

(iii)   If there is any foul (running with the ball, rough play, obstruction), a free throw is given to the opposite side.

(iv)   If the ball goes off, a throw-in is taken by a player of the opposite team.

(v)   Scoring is 2 points for a direct hit, one point if the defence accidentally knocks down the skittle.

3 **Free netball** – this game requires no boundaries or marking, just two netball posts. The teams may consist of any number, but are best divided into attackers, centres and defenders. Anyone can score from any position, and the basic rules described previously provide the necessary guidelines for the activity.

4 **Hoopball** – this can be played using an improvised court divided into two or even three areas. Teams may be given positions similar to those of netball, with restrictions on their playing areas. One child from each team stands on a bench or chair at one end of the court (the end towards which the player's team will be shooting) holding a small hoop. To score, the shooters have to throw the ball through this hoop which is held horizontally above head height.

Players score by throwing the ball through their own hoop.

73 *Hoopball*

5 **Two-court dodge ball** – two teams are needed, and each stands in its own half of the area. The players use both hands to throw the ball, aiming to hit members of the opposing team

below the knees. Those who have been hit drop out. A throw-up decides which team shall start with the ball.

The game can continue until one team is the outright winner, or a set time limit is reached and the remaining players counted to establish the winning team. As a variation, more than one ball can be used to speed up the game and involve more children.

6 **Circle dodge ball** – one team forms a wide circle inside which the second team stands. Using one or more balls, the outer team tries to hit those inside the circle (as in 5, above). Once a time limit has been reached, or all the players have been hit, the two teams change places.

7 **Three-court dodge ball** – this is played with one or more balls and three teams, one of which stands in the central area and provides the target for the two outside teams. Players who have been hit join the side which hit them. The winning team is the one having most players at the end of the game.

8 **Team passing dodge ball** – using one ball and two chalk circles each one metre in diameter at either end of the playing area, the teams aim to hit an opponent standing in the circle. The ball must hit below the knee to score. The playing area can be divided lengthwise and children restricted to their own half of the court. The game is then played using the same rules as for skittle ball (see 2, above).

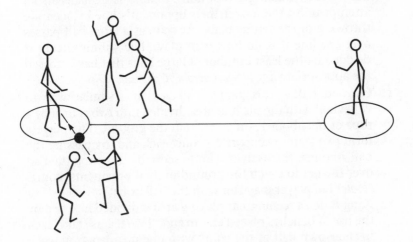

Score by hitting the opponent in the circle below the knee with the ball.

74 *Team passing dodge ball*

9 **Bombardment** – two teams of children are arranged as for 5, above, with additionally a row of skittles spaced out behind them. Each team has one or more balls at the start of the game and tries to knock down the opposing team's skittles while defending its own. As a variation, divide the area into four, and the two teams into shooters and defenders. The two defending teams stand just in front of their own skittles while the shooters stand on opposite sides in the two central areas. When a defender gets the ball, it is passed back to the team's shooters over the heads of the opposing team.

75 Bombardment

10 **Ball bombardment** – two teams each with several tennis balls stand behind lines at opposite sides of the indoor area. Equally spaced between these two lines is a row of large balls. At a signal, players aim at these large balls in an attempt to hit them over their opponent's line by accurate throwing of the tennis balls. As soon as a large ball passes over the line it is no longer in play. The winning team is decided by the least number of large balls that have crossed the appropriate line. (*See diagram 76 opposite.*)

11 **Ground ball** – this game is played in a similar way to volleyball with the playing area divided into two courts by a rope or net about 1.5 metres from the ground. The players form two teams occupying a court each and, by passing the ball amongst themselves, aim to score by throwing the ball over the net to touch the ground in their opponents' court. (*Note:* No player may run with the ball or bat it.)

12 **King Ball** – a rectangular playing area is divided into two by the use of benches placed end to end. Two teams stand each in their own half of the court with one member from each team, named the 'King', standing in the area behind his opponent's territory. One team starts with the ball and tries to throw it to their own 'King' behind their opponents' line

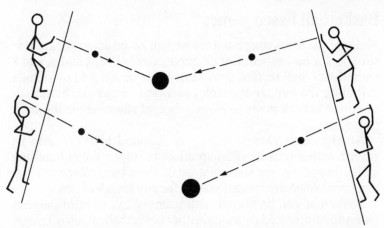

By throwing a small ball, players aim to knock the large balls over their opponent's line.

76 Ball bombardment

while preventing passes reaching their opponents' 'King'. Once a 'King' gains possession of the ball, he tries to hit an opponent with it below the knee. If he is successful, that player must join his own 'King'. The winning team is the first to put all opponents behind the line.

(*Note*: A throw-up at the start of the game can decide which team has the ball first, and the usual rules for netball then apply.)

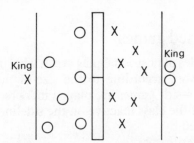

Teams try to pass the ball over to their own King who then aims to hit an opponent below the knee. When hit, a player joins his or her own King.

77 King Ball

Basketball based games

Many of the ideas suggested for netball based activities are also suitable for basketball. For example, games 1, 2, 3 and 4, and 8 from the netball section above can easily be adapted to include dribbling the ball. If available, basketball rings can be substituted for netball posts to allow rebound shooting off the back board.

All the other games, except 11 (Ground ball) can also be played with a basketball in an effort to improve ball handling skills. However, the static nature of these particular activities can prove too restricting if played for any length of time.

Basketball can be played with teams of five to eight players, using an improvised court and either basketball or netball rings. Teams can be even larger if substitution, which takes place after 5 fouls, is allowed. (The number of fouls can be reduced if it is wished to involve more children.) A jump ball between two players starts the game and players dribbling the ball use only one hand, never two. Once the ball is held, the same footwork rule which applies in netball comes into force. Two points are awarded for a basket and one for a free throw, which is generally given for fouls committed on opponents (e.g. barging).

In order to encourage team play, the 3 second rule can be introduced. This means that players cannot be in their opponents' free throw zone for more than 3 seconds when their team has the ball. Unless a court is permanently marked, a chalk line can indicate the approximate area.

Football based games

Because the rules of positional play are flexible in football, team numbers can vary according to the size of the playing area. Generally five-a-side games are played indoors, but this leaves the majority of the class inactive on the sideline. The situation can be improved by:
(a) having larger teams;
(b) substituting players who foul;
(c) timing to create many short games rather than two long ones, so that periods of inactivity are minimal;
(d) playing two or more games simultaneously across the space, involving all the children in small-sided games.
1 **Conventional football** can be played using a large lightweight or foam ball. Goals can be set up using skittles,

rounders posts, or benches on their sides. To score, the ball has either to pass between the two markers or to hit the flat side of the bench, whichever is appropriate.

For indoor games, the ball is restricted to waist height and may be played off the wall. If furniture or fixtures limit this particular move, additional benches laid on their sides and placed in front of the obstacles will provide an adequate flat surface.

If defending a bench or skittle goal, the goalkeeper can have a mat on which to kneel and throughout play should always have some part of the body in contact with it. However, a goal created by posts can be defended by a keeper who is standing.

The goalkeeper must stay on the mat. Players keep out of the semicircle.

78 Football

For more able children, a chalk semicircle round each goal can be introduced. Only the respective goalkeepers are allowed in this area. In order to encourage passing, each team is only permitted to make a shot at goal after the ball has been passed three times consecutively.

2 **Skittle ball** – instead of using the kind of goal suggested above, a skittle is set up and teams have to hit their opponents' skittle with the ball. (See netball section, page 93.)

3 **Crab football** – players have to move on all fours, and should not sit down. The ball is played using the feet, and goals are scored as described under 1, above. *(See diagram 79, page 100.)*

Players move on hands and feet only.

79 Crab football

These three games can also be played using a smaller ball (e.g. a tennis ball).

4 **Ball bombardment** – this can be played with any number of children who kick the ball instead of throwing it (see netball section, 10, above).

Volleyball based games

With a net or rope suspended down the centre of the hall or gymnasium, two or even three games can be played simultaneously. Courts can be divided by benches placed end to end. For games organised in this way, teams can be of four to six players.

A net hung across the area and the use of the technique of playing to the walls will enable more children to be involved in a game. Under such conditions, the recognised team number of six players can be considerably increased. During the early stages of volleyball it is quite usual for children to be rather static, and this coupled with the extended court provides an ideal opportunity for larger groupings. Positions on court normally consist of two lines of three players each, with players rotating clockwise one place every time their side wins back the service. For larger teams using an extended court, the players can form three rows of three to four children (see diagram 80).

Whatever arrangements are made, the game follows the basic rules given below.

(a) Serve – from the right-hand corner, outside the court. If the ball hits the net, it is a fault.

(b) Score – points are only scored when serving (as in badminton).

(c) Out-of-play – a ball that touches the ceiling, wall, or floor is out-of-play (unless a one bounce rule is introduced initially).

(d) Foul – players may not touch the ball twice consecutively, or touch the net. The maximum number of touches before the

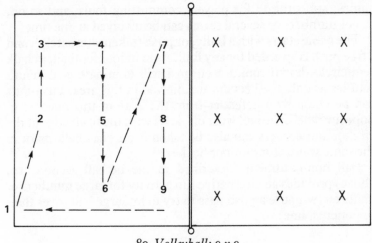

80 Volleyball: 9 x 9

ball must cross the net is three. It is also a foul if a ball is scooped or carried as opposed to being given a clean hit.

To promote passing and rallying in the early stages, the ball can be allowed to bounce once between each hit, enabling players to gain better control because they have time to position themselves correctly. For the child experiencing difficulty with serving, the ball may be thrown over.

Once a reasonable standard of play is established, the 'dig-set-smash' routine should provide the pattern of play where possible, with the opposing team's smashes blocked by the front row of players.

Hockey based games

For a game situation, a pudding ball tends to be the most suitable type as it does not bounce on rebounds as does a tennis or airflow ball. Because only a push pass (not a drive) is used to hit the ball, hands are always kept apart on the stick. As with football, rebound balls can be played, so it may be necessary to place benches on their sides to form boundaries.

The general organisation of indoor hockey is very similar to that for football. Both the conventional game and the skittle ball variation (see under netball section, 2, above) can be followed, with goalkeepers allowed to use their feet to stop and kick the ball.

Teams can consist of up to seven players (three forwards, three defences, one goalkeeper), and by introducing timed games, substitution for players committing fouls, and so on, larger numbers or several teams can be involved at one time.

The game starts with a bully, or push (taken alternately), and a free push is awarded for any foul. As in indoor football, a chalk semicircle drawn round each goal will eliminate goal-mouth scuffles as only the keepers are allowed in this area. Push-outs can be taken by a defender from the edge of this mark (e.g. opposite where the ball went off, level with the front edge of the circle), and corners can also be taken using the chalk mark in the same way as for outdoor hockey.

Ball bombardment (described in the netball section, 10, above) provides an alternative fun activity for large numbers of children (who use a push pass to try to hit large balls over their opponents' line).

Rugby based games

Any attempt to play Rugby football indoors will obviously have limitations, and if these are (a) no tackling and (b) no kicking, handling becomes of prime importance. Teams can vary in size according to the playing area; their aim is to ground the ball behind the opposing team's goal line in order to score a try. Tackling is carried out by touching the opponent with two hands below the waist. When so touched, the player in possession of the ball has to heel it back to a player behind him or her before passing can commence. If a team is successfully tackled three times, the ball is given to the opposing team and so the game continues. After a try is scored, the ball is given to the opposing team who have to start from their opponents' goal line. (*Note*: There is no forward passing.)

Cricket based games

Indoor cricket games should use a tennis, airflow or small foam ball, and if necessary the floor at the wicket should be protected by a mat. As the ball is a lightweight one, a plywood bat shape is more than adequate for indoor work.

1 **Spry** – this is a pairs cricket match, with five couples working with the same partner throughout. Pair 1 goes in and bats for two overs, counting runs scored and times dismissed. The score is then the difference between these two. Pair 2 consists of one who bowls and one who keeps wicket, Pair 3 is two umpires, Pair 4 fields on the off side, and 5 on the leg side.

At the end of two overs, the pairs rotate, and this pattern is repeated until each couple has experienced all the positions. The winners are the pair with the best average score.

2 **Non-stop A** – batsmen run between wickets whenever the ball is hit (tip and run rules). All the batting takes place at one end and the bowling at the other (it may be underarm or overarm). Dismissals occur through being bowled, caught, or run out, the last being allowed only at the wicket-keeper's end. The only pause in the bowling is between innings.

3 **Non-stop B** – this is a simpler form of the previous game using one batsman who, having hit the ball, runs round a wicket or skittle positioned about 6 metres away to square leg, carrying his or her bat.

4 **Perpetual cricket** – this form of cricket follows the usual layout for the fielding team, but the method of play is quite different. The bowler uses an underarm action and the batsman strikes the ball (tennis or foam) with the palm of the hand. Whether the ball is hit or not the batsman must attempt a run, to a line beyond the bowler and back to cross

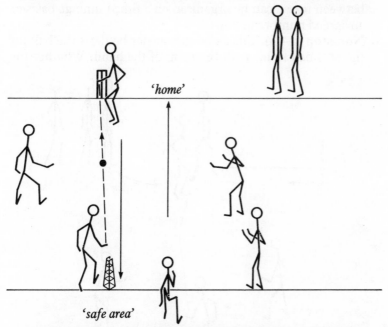

The bowler uses an underarm action. The batsman hits with the hand. Fielders try to touch the running batsman with the ball held in the hand.

81 Perpetual cricket

the batting line. As batsmen run, the fielders try to touch them with the ball (which must be in the fielder's hand and not thrown). Batsman can wait at the far line until another ball has been bowled, but no run is then scored. The bowler bowls continuously at the wicket which means that batsmen must follow one another quickly to the batting square. In this way, a batsman can be out without ever striking the ball.

Batsmen are out if they are:

(a) bowled out;
(b) touched with the ball while running between lines;
(c) caught out (the whole team is out on a catch).

The wicket for this game is created by a box or similar object.

5 **Long ball** – this is a variation on the previous game, using the same method of bowling and batting. However, the fielders try by throwing the ball to hit the batsmen below the knee to get them out. A run is scored when the batsman runs to the far line and back to 'home' again without being hit. As in 4, above, a small light ball should be used and competition between teams can be organised on a timed innings basis or an agreed number of bowls.

6 **Non-stop C** – for this game the bowler bounces the ball for the batsman to hit with the palm of the hand. Whether the

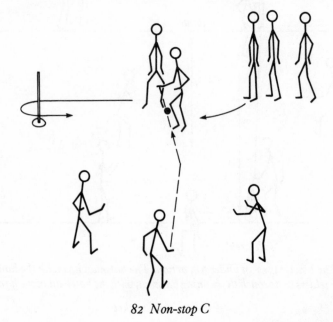

82 Non-stop C

ball is hit or not, the batsman has to run to the right, round a skittle about 4 metres away and back for the next bowl. Every time the bowler bowls, the batsman must complete a run even if he or she has missed the ball. Fielders always throw the ball immediately to the bowler, as a bowl that has bounced once and then is caught by the backstop gets the player out. With the bowler bowling continuously, batsmen have to change places quickly to prevent the incoming player being out before he or she has had a chance to get into position. A player continues to bat until caught or bowled out, and a point is scored for every run completed round the skittle. If a ball is hit well, or misfielded, more than one run can be attempted.

7 **Stoolball** – this offers a mixture of cricket and rounders, using a lightweight ball, any bat shape, and two wickets comprising 30 centimetre square boards attached to an upright post at approximately 1 metre from the floor. These two wickets and two batsmen are placed about 8 metres apart, with the bowler positioned in mid-wicket. Underarm bowls are aimed at the square, and after an over (6 bowls) another fielder takes a turn and bowls to the opposite wicket.

83 Stoolball

A batsman can be out in the following ways:
(a) bowled out (the ball hits the face of the wicket);
(b) caught;

(c) run out (the ball, thrown by a fielder, hits the wicket face
before the batsman can reach the wicket);

(d) by hitting his (her) own wicket with the bat.

For larger teams a tip and run method of play will speed up
the game, as will the retirement of any batsman scoring 15 runs.

Quoits based games

1 **Ring the quoit** – a game for any number of children divided
into two teams, with one player from each team at either end
of the playing area standing on a mat and holding a stick (a
rounders bat or post). Players are paired with an opponent
whom they mark. The game starts with a throw-up between
two opposing players, and to score the quoit must be passed
amongst the team (no moving is allowed when in possession
of the quoit) and eventually thrown to ring the post held by
the player on the appropriate mat. If an attempt to ring the
post is unsuccessful, a free pass is taken by the opposing team
from a position at the front of the mat.

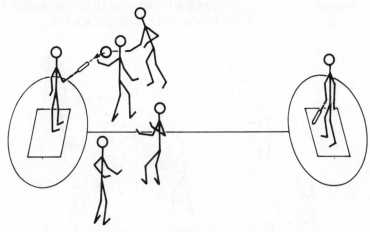

*Players try to throw the quoit to ring the bat being held by their own
team member on the mat.*

84 Ring the quoit

A variation which will prevent crowding is to divide the
court lengthwise, and to restrict players to their own area. A
semicircle, drawn round the player on the mat and which
cannot be entered by other players, increases the difficulty in
scoring.

For both these games the player on the mat must always stay on it. However, after there has been a score, the player can change places with another member of the team.

2 **Quoit pass** – two teams are arranged as for the previous game, but each player on the mat is replaced by a rounders post. The game proceeds in the same way and the teams score by ringing the post.

Rounders based games

Apart from the variations on the basic game of rounders, there are also numerous ways of combining other sports with this game. Most of these use four bases arranged in a square with a bowling and a batting square. The bases can be marked in various ways according to the particular game.

The general organisation of these games requires two teams whose members should all be given the opportunity of batting and fielding within the time allowed for the activity. To ensure that this is possible, games can be played in one of the following ways:

(a) a timed innings for each team;
(b) one hit per child (that is, one turn as batsman);
(c) a catch gets the whole team out.

Fielding positions should also be changed so that more than one player gains experience as bowler, backstop, and base fielder.

Throughout the following games, the batsman only has one bowl (unless it is a no ball) and must always run.

1 **Rounders** – played exactly as if out of doors, with four posts and the batsman using an open hand or a bat if a foam or airflow ball is used. (Players should always take the bat with them and not throw it down, which is hazardous for fielders.)
Players are out in the following ways:

(a) caught (the catch can be a rebound off the wall or ceiling);
(b) stumped out at the post to which they are running;
(c) body-stumped while running (by a fielder who has the ball in his or her hand);
(d) run out by the following batsman who forces a player to run on to an already stumped post.

With older, more able children, the rule of misfielding can also be applied – that is, if a ball is dropped after a post has been stumped, the stumping no longer applies and the batsman can run on.

2 **Danish rounders** – the organisation for this game is exactly as above, though the four bases can be marked simply by beanbags or by static players wearing bands. When a ball has been bowled, it is passed round the fielders at the four bases (always starting at first base) in an attempt to beat the batsman who is running round the bases at the same time. If the batsman beats the ball a rounder is scored. If the ball is dropped on its way round the bases it must be returned to first base and start again.

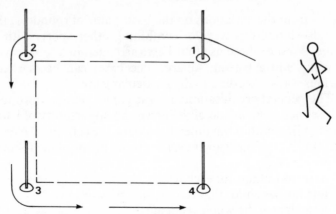

The batsman has to reach fourth base before the ball which is being thrown round the four bases.

85 Danish rounders

Batsmen are out if:
(a) the ball beats them to fourth base having been passed correctly round all the bases;
(b) a catch is taken (even a rebound off the wall or ceiling), when the whole team is out;
(c) a player intentionally hits the ball behind him (her).

3 **Mat rounders** – using four mats for bases, batsmen score a rounder every time they reach the fourth (last) base. The bowler throws the ball which the batsman tries to hit with the hand. Once the batsman has attempted a hit he or she starts running round the mats, stopping at any one. Fielders must get the ball back quickly to the bowler, who calls 'Stop!' At this point any batsmen running between the mats are out. Every time the ball is bowled, the batsmen must run at least one base. Batsmen can in fact overtake one another, or several can stop at the same mat.

4 **Bombardment mat rounders** – this is a variation of the previous game with a different way of getting out the batsmen. Any fielder can get the batsmen out by throwing the ball to hit them below the knee while they are running between mats. Fielders may not run with the ball, but have to pass it.

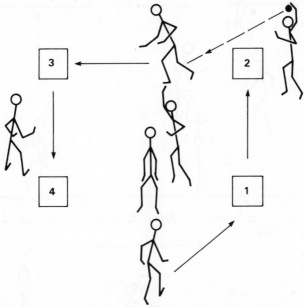

Fielders throw the ball to hit batsmen below the knee as they are running between mats.

86 *Bombardment mat rounders*

5 **Bombardmei rounders** – no posts or bases are required, only a safe are ı at the opposite end to the batsman. This safe area can be crated by a line drawn across the room about a metre from the wall. Once the batsmen have tried to hit the ball with their hands, they run to the opposite end of the hall to the safe area. Fielders, who must stand still when holding the ball, try to hit the running players below the knee to get them out. Batsmen only score on successfully returning to the batting end, and may only run when a ball has been bowled. *(See diagram 87, page 110.)*

6 **Four circle rounders** – for this, posts are replaced by mats, or chalk circles are drawn, and fielders arrange themselves outside the bases. The batsman receives the ball from an underarm bowl, catches it, and immediately throws it as far

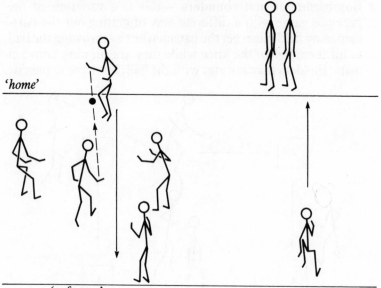

Fielders try to hit batsman below the knee when they are running between lines.

87 *Bombardment rounders*

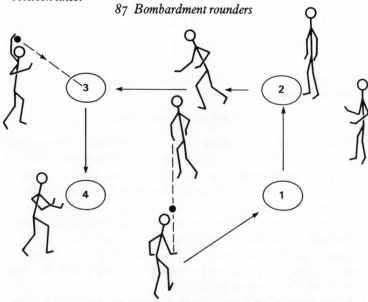

The batsman catches the bowl and throws the ball forwards into a space before trying to run round the circles. Fielders throw the ball to bounce in the circle to which the batsman is running.

88 *Four circle rounders*

as possible into a space in front of the batting square. When running for a rounder, batsmen must step on to or inside each base.

A batsman is out when:

(a) a throw is caught;

(b) the ball is thrown behind;

(c) the ball is bounced on to a base marker to which he or she is running;

(d) he or she runs on after the bowler has received the ball in the bowler's square.

Fielders should aim to throw the ball on to the nearest base, or return it to the bowler.

7 **Apparatus rounders** – the rules of 1, above, apply to this version of rounders, but the bases consist of four items of large gymnastic apparatus (box or horse, for example). When running for a rounder, the batsmen must cross the apparatus in the fastest way possible, and if stopping on the way round they must stand on the apparatus to be still in the game.

8 **Touch ball rounders** – similar scoring and methods of play to Danish rounders (see 2, above) are used in this variation, with the exception of the fielding. While the batsman runs round the posts, the fielders try to hit him or her below the knee with the ball. (Remember that fielders may not move when holding the ball.)

9 **Tunnel ball rounders** – this game uses a large ball which the batsman catches and throws forwards before running round the four bases without stopping. When the ball is fielded, all the other fielders line up behind the player with the ball who rolls it through their legs to the player at the back of the line. A rounder is scored if the batsman reaches fourth (last) base before the ball gets to the end of the tunnel. (*Note:* The teacher should call 'Stop!' when fourth base is reached.)

(*See diagram 89, page 112.*)

As a variation, a small ball hit with an open hand will provide a slightly different game.

10 **Archball rounders** – for this variation, the game proceeds as for tunnel ball rounders, above, but fielders pass the ball backwards overhead to the end of the line.

11 **Goal shooting rounders** – four bases are marked, and a netball post is placed outside the fourth base (unless a permanent netball or basketball ring is available). A shooter is appointed and stands near the ring.

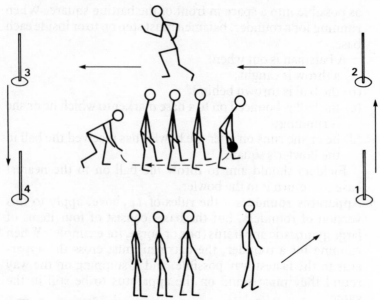

The batsman throws the ball forwards and then tries to run round all the posts before the fielders can complete one pass through the tunnel.

89 Tunnel ball rounders

The large ball is bowled for the batsman to catch and throw forwards before running round the bases. The fielders must catch and pass the ball to the shooter who attempts to score as many goals as possible before the batsman reaches fourth post. When fourth post is reached, the teacher calls 'Stop!'. The shooter should be changed frequently, and the team scoring the highest number of goals is the winner.

12 **Football rounders** – the method of play is similar to that described for 1, above, except that the bowler rolls a small ball along the ground which the batsman must kick forward with one foot. Fielders can kick or throw the ball to the bases and a rounder is scored in the usual way. Apart from catches, the batsman can be out in any of the ways listed under 1, above.

13 **Hockey rounders** – this is a version of rounders similar to the previous game, but all the players have a hockey stick. The bowler rolls the ball which the batsman stops and pushes into a space with the stick. Fielders may pass or dribble the ball, but have to use their hands to stump a post in order to get players out.

The ball is pushed by the batsman and dribbled or pushed by the fielders.

90 Hockey rounders

14 **Quoit Danish rounders** – an adapted version of 2, above, in which a quoit is substituted for a small ball. The quoit is thrown to the batsman who catches it and throws it forwards. Once it has been caught, it is passed round by the fielders as in Danish rounders, above.

15 **Beanbag Danish rounders** – an adapted version of 2, above, in which a beanbag is substituted for a ball or a quoit. The beanbag is caught and thrown forwards by the batsman, and the game proceeds as above.

6
Potted Sports

These types of indoor games are designed actively to involve large numbers of players in a variety of skills providing a competitive situation. They always prove popular among the children, and can easily and simply be adapted to suit the particular game the children are working on out of doors. Good organisation is essential, with each task being explained and demonstrated, but once the introduction has been given little effort on the part of the teacher is then necessary for the sports to run smoothly.

Groupings

According to the numbers and space available, the class is arranged into groups of four or six children. Numbers do not usually divide exactly and it may sometimes be necessary to have a group of three or five children. This does not really matter, and the problem can easily be overcome in one of the following ways:

(a) If the skill is an individual one, with children taking it in turn to attempt it, then the number in the group does not matter.
(b) If the skill involves partner work, the space can be filled by the teacher (the situation may only arise perhaps twice or three times throughout the sports period).
(c) If the teacher is unable to join in, then three children form a triangle and the score is made up by doubling that of one other pair in the group.
(d) If a group has an extra person, then a partner skill is tackled with three members of that group forming a triangle as in (c), with no additional points being added to those gained by the partners who have participated.

Scoring

Throughout the series each group is competing against the others, and by rotating each activity all the groups eventually attempt all the tasks. Every skill should be timed, and the teacher should use a whistle to start and stop the children. While the groups are working they should constantly count the number of successful attempts they make. If children work on an individual skill, such as shooting, one member of the group keeps a record of the actual goals scored. If the task involves partner work, each pair keeps its own score and at the end of the activity this is added to the scores gained by the other pairs in the group (unless of course odd numbers are involved – see above).

Between each timed activity the teacher records the score of every group. After all the tasks have been completed, the scores for the various activities are added together and the group with the highest number of points is the winner. From the scores it can be seen which group wins in each particular skill, and whether or not extra work is required in any specific area of a sport (indicated if all groups have poor results in any of the activities).

Timing

The amount of time allowed for attempting each activity will largely depend on two factors: (a) the total time available, and (b) the number of groups. As a guideline, generally anything between one and three minutes is acceptable. Perhaps younger children would benefit from a slight reduction in timing (e.g. a maximum of two minutes), but older children, particularly boys, are capable of greater endurance.

To ensure the smooth running of these enjoyable and useful activities, the teacher must be prepared. This means having the necessary skill practices already worked out, and being equipped with a stopwatch, score sheet, pencil and whistle. Before embarking on potted sports, a warm-up activity is still needed.

The selection of sports in this chapter have largely been arranged from specific games, which in many cases tend to involve either boys or girls. However, it is quite a simple matter to combine tasks from several different activities to provide suitable material for mixed groups. Moreover, once the teacher has experienced these kinds of learning practices the imagination can be triggered and variations and additional tasks relevant to the class's particular needs can be devised. Thus the choice of activity is extended even further.

For each sport, eight tasks are suggested; these can be used to cater for 32 or 48 children according to the size of the class. If a really large area of sports hall is available, groups can have up to eight members, or tasks can be repeated with a different size ball or a different shape of bat.

Activities leading to football

1 **Dodging** – players dodge in and out of ropes without touching them. If no ropes are available, children move in and out between members of their own group in the same way. Score one point for every successful attempt.

2 **Throw-in (overhead pass)** – players work in twos, using a suitable gap in a window ladder, or passing over a string or a high jump pole set at a suitable height. Score one point for every accurate throw-in caught by a partner.

3 **Dribbling** – individual children dribble in and out of bean-bags spaced on the floor. Score one point for every successful attempt.

4 **Push passing in twos** – spaced 3 or 4 metres apart (a uniform distance for all groups should be established by the use of existing lines on the floor or chalk marks), children complete as many passes as possible within the time allowed. Score one point for every accurate pass that a partner is able to stop.

5 **Heading in twos** – according to the age and ability of the children this skill can be tackled in one of the following ways:

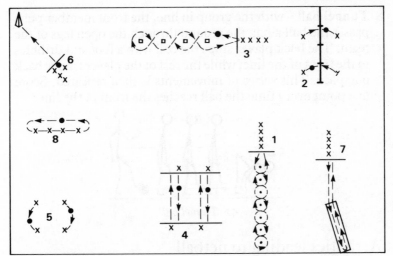

Indoor plan for the eight activities for football
1 *Dodging in and out of the ropes in both directions*
2 *Throw-in to a partner through a high space in the window ladder*
3 *Dribbling a football in and out of beanbags on the floor*
4 *Push passing a football to a partner*
5 *Heading the ball in twos*
6 *Kicking a stationary ball at a skittle*
7 *Running up and down an inclined bench*
8 *Tunnel ball*

91 *Potted sports: football*

(a) One child throws the ball into the air; a partner heads the ball back for a catch. Score one point for each successful attempt.

(b) Pairs try to keep a rally going, allowing one bounce between heading. Score one point for every consecutive header.

(c) Pairs try to keep a continuous rally going without the ball touching the floor. Score one point for every consecutive header, adding points to those already earned every time a new rally is started.

6 **Shooting** – using a push pass from a set line, each group member takes a turn at kicking a ball to hit or knock down a skittle. Score one point if the skittle is hit.

7 **Agility** – using an inclined bench (with one end attached to a wall bar), each group member in turn runs up the bench, touches the wall and runs down again. Score one point every time a successful run is completed.

8 **Tunnel ball** – with the group in line, the front member push passes the ball along the ground through the open legs of the team. The back player stops the ball with a foot and dribbles to the front of the line, while the rest of the players move back one pace. This series of movements is then repeated. Score one point every time the ball reaches the front of the line.

92 Tunnel ball

Activities leading to netball

1 **Passing in twos** – players use a chest, shoulder, overhead, or underarm pass through an appropriate gap in a window ladder or wall bars. Score one point for every ball successfully passed through the correct gap and caught by a partner.
2 **Bounce pass in twos** – pairs are spaced uniformly and bounce pass (a) using existing floor markings or chalk marks (b) under a lowered bar (c) into a hoop. Score one point for each accurate pass caught by a partner.
3 **Dodging** – one at a time, children dodge in and out of a line formed by children of their own group, or if ropes are available negotiate these without touching them. Score one point for every successful attempt.
4 **Shooting** – children take it in turn to shoot from a set marker, using netball or basketball rings according to availability. Score one point for every goal.
5 **Tunnel ball** – with the group in line, the ball is rolled through the open legs of the team by the front player. The back player picks it up and runs to the front of the line to repeat the procedure. Score one point each time the ball reaches the front of the line.
6 **Pepperpot** – children stand side by side, facing the person with the ball who, using any of the five main passes, throws the ball to each member of the team in turn, working from left to right along the line. The last player to catch the ball keeps it and runs to the front, while the front player joins the other end of the line (see diagram). Score one point every time the front player changes.

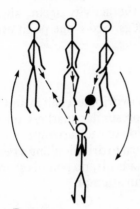

Pepperpot
This activity can be tried
using all the five passes.

Circle passing
All the passes can be used
for this activity.

93 *Potted sports: netball*

(*Note*: If the group is one person short, then one extra pass is made to the first person in the line. If one group has an extra player, then all the other groups have to make an extra pass.)

7 **Circle passing** – the groups each form a circle round the player with the ball which is thrown backwards and forward round the circle using any of the five main passes. When the ball reaches the starting point, the player who was first to receive it changes places with the centre player and passing continues as before. Score one point each time the centre player changes.

(*Note*: The same arrangements as in the previous activity apply if numbers in the groups are not exactly equal.)

8 **Under and over** – children form a line and the front player passes the ball through his or her open legs to the next player behind who passes it over the head, and so on down the line. When the ball reaches the end of the line, the last player runs

94 *Under and over*

with it to the front and begins the activity again, always starting by passing between the legs. Score one point every time the ball is at the front of the line.

Activities leading to hockey

1 **Dribbling** – players take it in turn to dribble a ball in and out of an arrangement of beanbags or similar markers on the floor. Score one point on completion of each attempt.
2 **Dribbling** (2) – players take it in turn to dribble along a bench top in both directions. If the ball falls off, no point is scored. Score one point for every successful attempt.

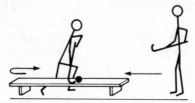

Dribbling along a bench in both directions

95 *Potted sports: hockey*

3 **Shooting** – children work from a specified line, aiming at (a) a skittle which has to be hit, or (b) a goal created by closely spaced skittles. Score one point when the attempt is successful.
4 **Scooping** – children work from a set line and take turns at scooping a stationary ball into a bucket or box laid on its side on the floor. Score one point every time the ball enters the container. As a variation, replace the container by a hoop, or use wall bars.

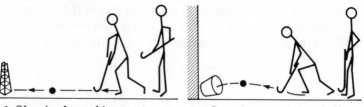

96 *Shooting by pushing a stationary ball at a target*

97 *Scooping a stationary ball into a container*

5 **Push pass in twos** – with pairs facing one another a set distance apart, the ball is passed backwards and forwards using a stick. (*Note*: The children must stop the ball before

pushing it back, to ensure that the ball does in fact travel in the correct direction.) Score one point for each accurate pass made to a partner.

6 **Kicking in twos** – children are spaced apart in pairs, and use their feet to attempt the same type of activity as 5, above. Score one point for each accurate return of the ball to the partner.

7 **Tunnel ball** – play in the same way as football skill 8 (see page 118), but players use a stick to pass and dribble the ball instead of the feet. Score one point every time the ball is at the front of the line.

8 **Pepperpot** – members of the group arrange themselves in similar positions to those described under netball skill 6 (page 118). Instead of throwing the ball, players push and stop using a stick, and the last player dribbles the ball out and takes the place of the front person. Score one point every time the front player changes.

Activities leading to Rugby

1 **Dodging** – children move in and out of ropes or posts without touching them. Score one point for every successful attempt. As a variation, try dodging carrying a ball.

2 **Dodging and passing** – children stand in a line side by side and pass the ball along the line to the end. The last player carries the ball and dodges in and out of all the team members to become the first player, and so the activity continues. (Ensure teams are always equally spaced out.) Score one point every time the ball reaches the front of the line.

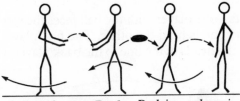

98 Potted sports: Rugby Dodging and passing

3 **Pick-up** – the team lines up at a set marker, facing a post, with a ball on the floor midway between the two. Each child takes it in turn to run, pick up the ball, continue round the post and replace the ball on its original spot before returning to the group. Then the next in line repeats the procedure. Score one point for each run. *(See diagram 99, page 122.)*

A player runs to pick up a stationary ball and takes it round a post before returning it to its mark.

99 *Pick-up*

4 **Circle passing** – children form a circle round a player with the ball which is passed backwards and forwards round the circle between the outer players and the one in the centre. When it returns to the first player, he or she changes places with the person in the middle, and passing continues. Score one point each time the centre player changes.

5 **Agility** – using an inclined bench, each group member takes a turn at running up the bench and touching the wall before running down again. Score one point for every successful run.

6 **Passing on the move** – while carrying a ball, each member of the team in turn runs round a skittle or post about 10 metres distant and returns, passing the ball to the next runner. Score one point for each completed run.

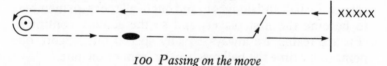

100 *Passing on the move*

7 **Line-outs** – one player with the ball faces the rest of the team who stand one behind the other. The first player throws the ball over the heads of the line to the back player who then has

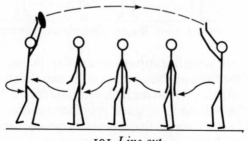

101 *Line-out*

to weave in and out of the team, carrying the ball, up to the front in order to repeat the task. (*Note:* To ensure uniform spacing, it is advisable to indicate on the floor where the front and back players should always be standing.) Score one point each time the back player reaches the front.

8 **Passing in twos** – pairs spaced uniformly apart (use floor markings) pass the ball to one another. Score one point for every ball caught.

Activities leading to basketball

All the activities suggested in the netball section of this chapter (see pages 118–20) can just as easily be used for basketball. However, the types of pass used in some of the skills need to be confined to chest, bounce, and overhead (the three passes most commonly used in basketball).

In addition to the eight ideas adapted from netball, there are listed below suggestions for five extra practices based on hand dribbling which can be included.

1 **Dribbling** – players take it in turn to dribble the ball round a skittle and back to the starting place, ready for the next person to complete the same course. Score one point for each run.

2 **Dribbling** (2) – children take it in turn to dribble in and out of beanbags or similar markers on the floor. Score one point for each run. As a variation, instead of using floor markers, children dribble in and out of their own team members who are spaced equally apart. Score one point for each completed individual run.

3 **Tunnel ball** – the group members stand one behind the other so that the front person can roll the ball through the open legs of the team to the back person who then dribbles the ball up to the front of the line so that the sequence of moves can be repeated. Score one point each time the ball reaches the front of the line.

4 **Overhead** – the group members stand as for tunnel ball, but the ball is passed over the heads of each player to the back of the line, and then dribbled up to the front so that the action can be repeated. Score one point every time the ball reaches the front of the line. (*See diagram 102, page 124.*)

5 **Shooting** – each child in turn dribbles the ball from a marker about 5 metres away from the basketball ring and tries to score a goal. Once the goal is scored, the player dribbles back

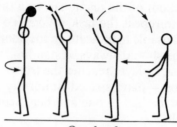

Overhead
The back player has to dribble the ball to the front of the team.

102 Potted sports: basketball

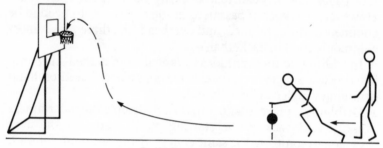

103 Dribbling and shooting

to the marker for the next child to take a turn. Score one point
for each goal.

Activities leading to table tennis and stoolball

1 **Bouncing** – each member of the group works individually,
using a bat and ball to try to establish a high number of
bounces on the floor. If a ball is missed or hit off course,
scoring stops and only continues when the bouncing sequence is re-started. (*Note:* Allow only *one* bounce between
each hit.) Score one point for every correct bounce.
2 **Batting** – members of the group work individually as each
child tries to keep a ball in the air by hitting it with a bat.
Score one point for each hit that does not touch the floor. As a
variation, the skill can be made simpler by allowing the ball to
bounce once between each hit.
3 **Batting in twos** – pairs spaced equally apart on markers bat
the ball to one another, allowing it to bounce once between
each hit. Score one point for each ball hit accurately.

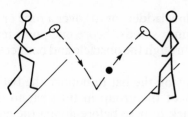

104 Batting in twos

4 **Batting in twos** (2) – using a wall target (a chalk circle or square), and batting the ball alternately, pairs aim to hit the target allowing a bounce between each return. Score one point each time the target is hit.

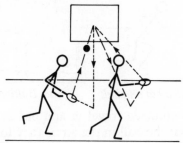

Each return is hit at the target and only bounces on rebounding from the wall.

105 Batting in twos (2) – aiming for a target on the wall

5 **Batting in twos** (3) – this is a slightly more advanced version of 3, above. The pairs not only have to aim the ball back for their partner to hit, but also hit it (a) over two stacked benches, or (b) over a lowered bar or beam, or (c) through a

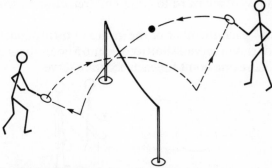

Each ball returned should bounce only on the opponent's side of the net (as in tennis).

106 Batting in twos (3) – over an improvised net

gap in a window ladder, or (d) over a rope or high jump pole attached to jump stands. Score one point for every hit that goes over or through the obstacle and bounces for a partner to hit.

6 **Dribbling** – using the bat to bounce the ball while moving, each member of the group in turn has to dribble round a skittle and back to base before giving the equipment to the next person in line for the task to be repeated. Score one point for each trip.

7 **Dribbling (2)** – as 6, above, but players weave in and out of posts or beanbags spaced out on the floor. Score one point for each successful run.

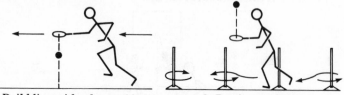

107 Dribbling with a bat and ball   *108 Batting on the move*

8 **Batting (2)** – children travel in and out of obstacles (as 7, above), but bat the ball in the air as they follow the course. Score one point *only* if the circuit is completed without the ball touching the floor.

Activities leading to tennis and badminton

Note: If available, small foam balls used with badminton or plastic rackets will prove easier than tennis equipment for the younger or smaller child to handle. Also stray foam balls present less of a hazard to other children close by than other kinds.

1 **Serving** – each member of the group in turn stands on a set line and tries to serve a shuttlecock into a hoop about 4 metres away. Score one point for each accurate serve.

109 Racket, ball and shuttlecock – badminton serving

2 **Accuracy** – from a set line, each member of the group takes a turn at hitting a ball with a racket, aiming for a wall target. Score one point for each accurate shot.

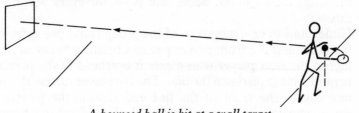

A bounced ball is hit at a wall target.

110 Accuracy

3 **Hitting in twos** – pairs face one another a set distance apart and hit a shuttlecock to one another in order to establish a rally. Score one point for each hit.

4 **Hitting in twos (2)** – work as in 3, above, but the task is made more difficult for the players by the introduction of a 'net' (either a rope or a high jump bar attached to jump stands). Score one point for each hit over the 'net'.

5 **Hitting in twos (3)** – using a ball and rackets, children work in pairs to maintain a rally, letting the ball bounce once between each hit. Score one point for each hit.

6 **Hitting in twos (4)** – as in 5, above, children work in pairs using rackets and a ball. The difficulty of the task is increased by the introduction of a 'net' (rope or high jump bar) over which the ball must go before it bounces. Score one point for every accurate return over the net (the ball must have bounced only once before it was hit).

7 **Batting** – children take it in turn to run about 4 metres to a skittle and back while using a racket to hit a ball in the air. Score one point for each run.

8 **Dribbling** – children take it in turn to dribble in and out of markers on the floor and back to base while using a racket to bounce the ball on the floor. Score one point for each completed turn.

Miscellany: activities using small equipment

Beanbags

1 **Tunnel ball** – the front player slides the beanbag along the floor between the open legs of the team members to the back player, who runs to the front of the group and repeats the

pattern. Score one point each time the beanbag reaches the front of the line.

2 **Aiming** – from a set line, players take turns at throwing beanbags into a hoop. Score one point for every accurate throw.

3 **Under and over** – members of the group stand one behind the other and the front player passes a beanbag between the legs to the next player who passes it overhead to the player behind, and so on down the line. The last player runs with the beanbag to the front of the line and repeats the pattern, always starting with a pass between the legs. Score one point every time the beanbag reaches the front of the line.

4 **Running** – with a beanbag balanced on the head, children take it in turn to run to a skittle and back to base. Score one point for every completed run.

5 **Jumping** – with a beanbag held between the knees, members of the group take turns in jumping to a skittle and back to base. Score one point for every completed run.

6 **Throwing in twos** – pairs throw a beanbag quickly and accurately to one another (a) across a distance of 3 to 4 metres, or (b) through an appropriate gap in a window ladder, or (c) using one hand only. Score one point for every accurate throw caught.

7 **Pepperpot** – set netball section 6 (page 118) for method of play and scoring.

Quoits

1 **Passing in twos** – children work with a partner to throw a quoit (a) across a distance of 3 to 4 metres, or (b) through an appropriate gap in wall bars or a window ladder, or (c) over an improvised net, or (d) using one hand only. Score one point for every accurate throw caught.

2 **Aiming** – children take it in turn to roll a quoit at a skittle from a set line. Score one point for every hit.

3 **Accuracy** – from a set position, members of the group take turns at throwing a quoit to hook over a rounders post. Score one point for each successful attempt.

4–6 **Tunnel ball**, **Under and over**, and **Pepperpot** can be organised using quoits in exactly the same way as suggested for beanbags under 1, 2, and 7 in the previous section.

Tennis or foam balls

1 **Bouncing** – group members work individually using a hand to bounce the ball on the floor. Score one point for every bounce.

2 **Bouncing in twos** – players bounce the ball backwards and forwards to one another across a 3 to 4 metre gap. Score one point for every bounce caught by a partner.

3 **Batting** – group members work individually using a flat hand to try to keep the ball off the ground by hitting it up in the air. Score one point every time the ball is hit in the air.

4 **Throwing in twos** – pairs try to throw and catch a ball accurately over a short distance, using only one hand. Score one point for each throw caught one-handed.

5 **Throwing in twos (2)** – children throw the ball underarm to a partner through a waist-high gap in a window ladder. Score one point for every accurate throw.

6 **Aiming** – using an underarm or overarm throw, members of the group take turns to try to hit a wall target. Score one point for every accurate throw.

7 **Accuracy in twos** – passing in pairs, children aim to get the ball to bounce in a hoop or similar target placed between them on the floor. Score one point for every accurate pass.

Circuits

When gymnastic apparatus is available, it is possible to create, for the older boys in particular, activities resembling circuits, which can be organised on lines similar to potted sports. However, care should be taken to ensure that the tasks are not over-demanding, and that they do not involve any unnecessary safety risks. For the introduction of this type of variation, the teacher in charge should be qualified in the use of the apparatus, and preferably a specialist (for the reasons given above).

Conclusion

The general aim throughout the six chapters of this book has been to provide a comprehensive guide which the class teacher can easily understand, giving quick reference for selecting activities relevant to particular requirements (bearing in mind age of pupils, ability, conditions, equipment, size of class and sport to be practised). An additional objective has been to develop vital skills, team co-operation, spatial awareness, healthy competition and sportsmanship within a safe environment, providing a sound basis for the major and minor games played in much larger areas.

For the more complicated or unusual games, additional instructions given in diagram form help to keep planning and preparation to a minimum – a great advantage, because inclement weather can strike suddenly, without prior warning.

The vast collection of games, skills and activities described has been carefully compiled in an attempt to give as much flexibility as possible, so that pupils of a wide range of ages and abilities can be profitably involved in activity whatever the limitations of available indoor conditions. Even if there is no equipment to hand, many of the team games can also be played substituting tightly-rolled socks for the ball.

For specialists, too, this collection could prove a useful source of ideas to be elaborated upon, or could suggest new variations on games already used. Thus the teacher's repertoire is extended, and the compact list of many activities can suggest some which have perhaps been long forgotten.

Finally, it should be remembered that the greater part of the material is multipurpose and can easily be adapted to form a basis for outdoor lessons.

List of Suitable Equipment

BALLS
airflow, tennis, pudding, volleyballs, basketballs, foam balls
(tennis to football size and preferably in the three different
bounce qualities), footballs (sizes 3–5), lightweight plastic balls
(sizes 3–5), netballs (sizes 3–5), Rugby (sizes 4–5)

BANDS
at least four sets of 10 in different colours

BATS
plywood cut-out shapes – cricket, padder tennis, stoolball,
table tennis; rounders (plastic or wood)

BEAN BAGS
a variety of colours

CHALK
playground blocks

HOOPS
wooden, or tubular plastic

QUOITS

RACKETS
badminton, tennis, short-handled plastic

SKIPPING ROPES
with or without handles

SKITTLES
wooden, plastic, and plastic-coated wire

STICKS
hockey, polypropylene, shinty, unihoc

STORAGE CONTAINERS
wooden boxes, plastic crates, plastic-coated wire baskets, bags,
nets

Cross-referenced Table
of Activities

Equipment and Sport related to:	Individual Skills Chapter 2	Partner Skills Chapter 3	Small Team Games and Group Activities Chapter 4	Large Team Games Chapter 5	Potted Sports Chapter 6
Basketball	21–2	54–5 78–9	64, 66 78–9	98	123–4
Bat and ball	25–6	44–5	64 83–5	see cricket 102–6	124–6
Beanbag	24–5	51	63, 66	113	127–8
Cricket	see tennis ball skills 16–19, 25–6	52–4	86–9	102–6	
Football	20	36–40	64, 65, 66	98–100 112	116–18
Hoop	24	51–2	63		
Netball	21	40–2	64, 66–72	92–7, 111	118–20
Quoit	25	51	63, 66	106–7, 113	128
Racket and ball or shuttlecock (tennis, badminton)	26	45	65 85–6		126–7
Rounders	see tennis ball skills 16–19, 25–6	55–6	90	107–13	
Rugby	29–30	56–8	76–8	102	121–3
Skipping rope	23–4	50	63–4		
Stick and ball (hockey)	26–8	45–9	64–5 73–6	101–2 112	120–1
Tennis or foam ball	16–19	31–6	62, 66	See rounders 107–11	129
Volleyball	22–3	42–4	79–83	100–1	

Glossary of Terms

block (*volleyball*)   jumping high at the net with arms stretched upwards in an attempt to stop an opponent's efforts to smash (see below).

dig (*volleyball*)   striking a volleyball upwards using the lower inside area of both forearms.

dribble (i) *hockey* pushing a controlled ball along the ground using a hockey stick.   (ii) *football* using the sides of the feet to propel a controlled ball along the ground.   (iii) *basketball* using the fingertips to bounce a ball along the ground.

grub kick (*Rugby*)   kicking a Rugby ball along the ground.

line-out (*Rugby*)   players form a line facing a player who throws a Rugby ball above their heads for them either to jump and catch or to tip to another player.

push pass (i) *hockey* passing a ball along the ground by placing the stick-head against the ball and pushing forwards with the lower (the right hand) of the two hands holding the stick. (ii) *football* using the side of the foot to pass the ball along the ground.

scoop (*hockey*)   lifting a hockey ball into the air using the head of the stick.

set (*volleyball*)   volley (see below) action to place the ball high in the air close to the net for smashing (see smash, below).

smash (*volleyball*)   jumping at the net, using an open hand to strike a volleyball down into the opponent's court.

trapping (*football*)   receiving and stopping a ball so that it is under control.

try (*Rugby*)   grounding a Rugby ball behind the opponents' goal line.

two-touch passing (*football*)   using one touch to control a ball, and a second to pass it.

volley (*volleyball*)   stretching arms above the head and using the fingertips to push a volleyball up into the air.

Example Lesson Plan 1

Suggested plan for a mixed class of eight-year-olds, based on hand striking skills using small balls (tennis or foam).

Equipment: 1 ball per child, plus a stick of chalk for the teacher

(a) Introductory activity – tag games

    Example   Ball tag (page 8, 10)

                  Partner tag with a small ball (page 8, 11)

(b) Individual skills practices

    Example   Tennis or foam ball skills (page 16, (a))

                  Children must use both their right and left hands to

        (i) bounce the ball on the floor;

        (ii) bat the ball into the air using a flat palm;

        (iii) bat the ball against a wall or similar surface, allowing it to bounce at least once between each return.

  Partner skills practices

    Example   Batting with a partner (page 33, (b))

                  Batting the ball alternately with a partner, again encouraging the use of both right and left hands, with an increased element of difficulty introduced by the use of floor targets.

(c) Game

    Example   1 v 1 (page 33)

                  Using an existing line on the floor, or a chalk mark, two children face one another across the line and try to hit the ball over it, allowing it to bounce once between each hit. By playing in a similar way to table tennis, a simple game may be developed, with points scored if the ball fails to bounce over the agreed line, or if the player fails to return it.

Example Lesson Plan 2

Suggested plan for a class of 36 twelve-to-thirteen-year-old girls, based on netball-type skills and activities

Equipment: 36 bands, 18 netballs, 6 benches

(a) Introductory activity – tag games
      Example   Tail tag (page 8, 5)
                    Partner tail tag (page 8, 6)

(b) Individual skills practices
      Example   Footwork skills (page 15, (b), (c), (d))

    Partner skills practices
      Example   Dodging and marking (page 41)
                    Partner work with a netball – static accurate passing, using a specified example (chest and bounce pass). This restricted skill should quickly be developed to incorporate footwork practice by placing the pass beyond the partner's immediate reach, thereby forcing the player to move in order to control and catch the ball.

(c) Group practices
      Example   Piggy-in-the-middle, or 2 v 1 – using the two passes practised with a partner (page 69, (b))
                    Pivoting and passing in fours (page 71, (a))
                    2 v 2 (page 71, (b))

(d) Game
      Example   Captain Ball for teams of six to ten players. Two or even three games can be played simultaneously across the indoor area (page 92, 1).

Mini-games

Junior versions of several major games have now emerged, enabling younger children to participate in recognised team games using simplified rules and smaller courts and pitches.

These mini-games offer a very useful transition from skills activities to the major sports, and full details can be obtained from the addresses below.

Short Tennis
Lawn Tennis Association, Barons Court, West Kensington, London W14 9EG

Mini-Rugby
Rugby Football Schools' Union, Whitton Road, Twickenham, Middlesex, TW1 7RQ

Mini-basketball
English Mini-basketball Association, The Greneway School, Garden Walk, Royston, Hertfordshire, SG8 7JF

Five-a-side Soccer
English Schools' Football Association, 4a Eastgate Street, Stafford, ST16 2NQ

Additional addresses

The Sports Council, 70 Brompton Road, London SW3 1EX

National Council for Schools' Sports, 99 Holly Walk, Enfield, Middlesex, EN2 6QB

Hockey Association, 70 Brompton Road, London SW3 1HB

English Schools' Volleyball Association, 91 Shipley Fields Road, Shipley, West Yorkshire.

English Schools' Netball Association, 41 View Drive, Dudley, West Midlands, DY2 7TO

All England Netball Association, 70 Brompton Road, London SW3 1HD

General Index